Edward W. Blyden

Liberia's offering

Being addresses, sermons, etc.

Edward W. Blyden

Liberia's offering

Being addresses, sermons, etc.

ISBN/EAN: 9783741195426

Manufactured in Europe, USA, Canada, Australia, Japa

Cover: Foto ©Andreas Hilbeck / pixelio.de

Manufactured and distributed by brebook publishing software (www.brebook.com)

Edward W. Blyden

Liberia's offering

LIBERIA'S OFFERING:

BEING

Addresses, Sermons, etc.

BY

REV. EDWARD W. BLYDEN.

NEW-YORK:
JOHN A. GRAY, PRINTER, STEREOTYPER, AND BINDER,
FIRE-PROOF BUILDINGS,
CORNER OF FRANKFORT AND JACOB STREETS.
1862.

HOPE FOR AFRICA:

A DISCOURSE

DELIVERED IN THE PRESBYTERIAN CHURCH, SEVENTH AVENUE, NEW-YORK,
JULY 21, 1861.

INTRODUCTION.

The contents of this volume will have nothing of the interest connected with travels or descriptive scenery. They are chiefly essays prepared for special occasions, expressive of the Author's views of the rights, duties, and hopes of the African race.

This small contribution to the literary wealth of Liberia, has been made in the hope of thus attracting to the Liberia College, in which the Author is a Professor, the favor of some who may have leisure and curiosity to examine it.

The prospect of Africa's future civilization, and of her taking rank among the advanced countries of the world, thus vindicating the oneness of origin from the first Adam, and of interest in the second Adam, may well stimulate all her children to the boldest efforts.

The Author in putting forth this small volume, feels assured that he has been actuated more by a desire to contribute something to the credit of the African race, to which he entirely belongs, and of the Republic of Liberia, with which, from choice, after twelve years' residence, he is fully identified, than by any vanity of appearing as an author. At the earnest suggestion of friends, to whose judgment he reluctantly defers, he introduces "LIBERIA'S OFFERING" with the following brief

Biographical Sketch.

My native place is St. Thomas, one of the Danish West-India Islands, where I was born August 3, 1832. I was blest with the care of pious parents. To the influence of my excellent and devoted mother, who is still alive, more than to any other earthly cause, can I trace whatever literary tastes and religious aspirations I possess.

In 1842, my father removed his family to Porto Cabello, Venezuela, and remained two years, returning to St. Thomas, in 1844. While residing in Venezuela, I learned to speak the Spanish language.

On my return to St. Thomas, I was apprenticed to the tailoring business, with a provision allowing me to attend school in the morning and the shop in the afternoon, and so continued for five years.

In 1845, Rev. John P. Knox, now pastor of a Presbyterian Church at Newtown, Long Island, came to St. Thomas and took charge of the Reformed Dutch Church. With others of my companions I became a member of a Bible-class under his instruction, and thus was formed a friendship which was of great benefit to me, and gave a turn to all my life. I was fond of composition and often indulged myself in attempts in that way. I was accustomed to take copious notes of his sermons, which especially attracted his attention, and led him to encourage me to prepare for the ministry, after I had formally joined his church, in which I had been baptized and brought up.

In 1850, when Mrs. Knox was about to return to the United States he encouraged me to come also, with the hope of securing for me admission to one of the colleges in this country. I found, however, the deep-seated prejudice against my race, exercising so controlling an influence in the institutions of learning, that admission to them was almost impossible.

Discouraged by the difficulties in my path, I proposed to return to St. Thomas, and abandon the hope of an education, when I received from Mrs. Knox a letter so full of interest in my welfare, and so urgent that I should still strive to become fitted for usefulness in the Christian ministry, and render my life useful to Africa, that I relinquished my purpose of returning to my parents. I decided to accept of the offer of the New-York Colonization Society to furnish me a passage to Liberia, in hopes to enjoy the advantages of the Alexander High School, then beginning its noble work, at Monrovia, the capital of the Republic.

By the Liberia packet from Baltimore, December 21, 1850, I was safely conveyed to the continent of my fathers and my race, reaching Monrovia, January 26, 1851. Arriving in Liberia, an entire stranger, without a single letter of introduction, I was received with great kindness by the people. Especially do I remember the cordial welcome and hospitable treatment extended to me by Mr. B. V. R. James and his family.

After a slight acclimation, I was, by the kindness of the Presbyterian Missionary Board, accepted as a student in the Alexander High School under charge of Rev. David A. Wilson, who carefully instructed me and others of my class-mates in Latin and Greek, as well as the usual lessons in Geography and Mathematics. The Hebrew language, not being embraced in the course of studies in the Alexander High School, I took up the study of it myself, and devoted for some time all my leisure hours to it; being anxious to read the entire Scriptures in the original languages, especially those passages of the Old Testament which have reference to the African race.

Three years after my admission to the school, during a visit for his health which Mr. Wilson made to the United States, I was placed in charge of some of the classes. While thus engaged in my first efforts at teaching, I was appointed by President Roberts, Editor of the *Liberia Herald*, which, without allowing it to interfere with my duties in the school, I conducted for one year.

After the return of Mr. Wilson, I continued to assist him from time to time as his health seemed to require it; and, in 1858, on his retirement, on account of the illness of his family, I was placed in full charge of the Alexander High School, where I continued teaching until 1861, when I was elected Professor of Greek and Latin in Liberia College.

It was under the ministry of Rev. Mr. Knox in St. Thomas, that I made a profession of religion. Ever looking forward to the ministry, I was *finally*, after the usual examinations, licensed and ordained by the Presbytery of West-Africa, in the year 1858.

In the early part of 1861, in order to recruit my impaired health, I made a visit to England and Scotland; thence I went to Canada, visited Niagara Falls, and spent a few weeks in the United States. While in England I was privileged to form the personal acquaintance of Lord Brougham, to whom I had the honor of presenting a walking-cane on behalf of the young men of Liberia; of Right Honorable W. E. Gladstone, and Rev. Henry Melvill, Principal of East-India College. With these gentlemen I had previously been in correspondence from Liberia. I was also shown great hospitality and kindness by Samuel Gurney, Esq., M.P., Gerard Ralston, Esq., and Thomas Hodgkin, M.D., of London, and by Rev. Drs. Guthrie and Johnston, of Edinburgh. By the last-named gentleman I had the honor of being presented to the United Presbyterian Synod, then in session in Edinburgh, at the same time that Rev. Dr. George B. Cheever of New-York City was introduced.

The Presbytery of West-Africa during their session, December,

1860, elected me their Commissioner to the General Assembly of the Presbyterian Church, (O. S.,) in the United States, which met in the city of Philadelphia, in May, 1861, but my delay in Europe prevented my enjoying the privilege of being the first black representative from Africa in that distinguished body.

Returning to Liberia in the autumn of the year, I was induced to accept the appointment from the Government, as Commissioner to the descendants of Africa in the United States and the West-Indies, to give information of Liberia, and invite them to a home in that country. In the prosecution of this mission, I arrived in this country, via England, in the month of May last.

The reader will see in this brief record, the kind leadings of that Providence which, from an obscure condition, in a distant island, has taken me on to my present position, without any special merit of my own. Friends and helpers have arisen in all my path, to all of whom I am a debtor for unmerited kindness, and whom I shall not cease to remember with gratitude while life lasts.

I ought not to close without adding a few words about my home in Africa. After twelve years' residence there, I have this summer made a filial visit to my aged mother, to feel once more her warm embrace. I found a most cordial welcome and unexpected honors among my former friends. The *New-York Colonization Journal* for October makes the following note of my visit to St. Thomas:

HONORED AT HIS HOME.

We learn that Professor Blyden, of the Liberia College, who is a native of St. Thomas, and, after an absence of twelve years in Liberia, has this summer been to visit his mother and friends, was received with very great respect and kindness. He filled the pulpit of the Dutch Church at St. Thomas, frequently, and always had crowded audiences.

His official character as a Commissioner of Liberia, to make known the advantages for honor and usefulness which that Republic presented, enhanced the interest with which his modest circular, setting forth with brevity the facts in the case, was received. Hundreds there and in the Tortugas Islands expressed a desire to emigrate to Liberia, to participate in its privileges, and partake of its noble duties toward Africa. A few were so much in earnest as to start at once. We proposed to quote several articles from the *St. Thomas Tidende*, but the papers have been borrowed and not returned in time. The young men of St. Thomas made a fund, and publicly presented Mr. Blyden with a tangible evidence of their regard, in the form of a silver flower-vase and plate, and other useful articles, of which we find the following brief notice in the *Tidende*, August 28d:

TESTIMONIAL TO REV. E. W. BLYDEN.

"We learn that on the evening of the twenty-second instant, a deputation of gentlemen waited on Rev. Edward W. Blyden, at his residence, and presented to him, on behalf of a large number of his fellow-townsmen, a very valuable testimonial, accompanied with a beautifully written address, expressive of the great pleasure which his visit to his native land has generally afforded, and of the warm appreciation felt by his countrymen of his efforts in the sacred cause of Africa's evangelization and regeneration. We trust that the presence in our town of the reverend gentleman may act as a stimulus upon his former associates and acquaintances, urging them to attempt great things for the outraged land with whose interests he has identified himself, and which is now attracting so largely the attention of the civilised world. It is gratifying to us to know that our little Island has furnished one to take a part in the great work of opening Africa to civilization, to which savans and philanthropists are hastening from Europe and America to devote themselves."

A society was formed called the "St. Thomas Liberia Association," composed of the most prominent men of the Island, who at once raised a fund and forwarded to the United States fifty dollars, to purchase maps, books, and periodicals concerning Liberia. It must be most gratifying to Professor Blyden to receive such tokens of hearty good-will and high appreciation from the people of his early home.

My heart is in Liberia, and longs for the welfare of Africa. An African nationality is the great desire of my soul. I believe nationality to be an ordinance of nature; and no people can rise to an influential position among the nations without a distinct and efficient nationality. Cosmopolitism has never effected any thing, and never will, perhaps, till the millennium. God has "made of one blood all nations of men," but he has also "determined the bounds of their habitation."

Liberia is a beautiful tropical country, teeming with the rich fruits of a perpetual summer, with mountains and valleys, and rivers and brooks, "well-watered every where as the garden of the Lord." In all these respects she can scarcely be surpassed.

Her civil, political, religious and social advantages, however, are her chief attraction. No community can have more perfect religious liberty. Republican government is nowhere more thoroughly carried out. No social disadvantage is felt by any descendant of Africa on account of color. The moment a colored man from America lands in Liberia, he finds the galling chains of caste falling from his soul, and he can stand erect, and feel and realize that he is indeed a man.

For myself and children I desire no wider field of labor and no greater privileges than I enjoy in that country. And could my voice reach every descendant of Africa in America, I would say to him: "Come away from the land of caste and oppression, to the freedom of our young Republic!" Come help us build up a Nationality in Africa.

The reader, I trust, will pardon the seeming egotism of this narrative, inseparable from the very nature of the composition, and be lenient to this "Offering" from Liberia.

EDWARD W. BLYDEN.

New-York, October 21, 1862.

CONTENTS.

		PAGE
1.	HOPE FOR AFRICA,	4
2.	VINDICATION OF THE AFRICAN RACE,	31
3.	THE CALL OF PROVIDENCE, ETC.,	67
4.	INAUGURAL ADDRESS AT THE INAUGURATION OF LIBERIA COLLEGE,	95
5.	EULOGY ON REV. JOHN DAY,	127
6.	A CHAPTER IN THE HISTORY OF THE AFRICAN SLAVE-TRADE,	151

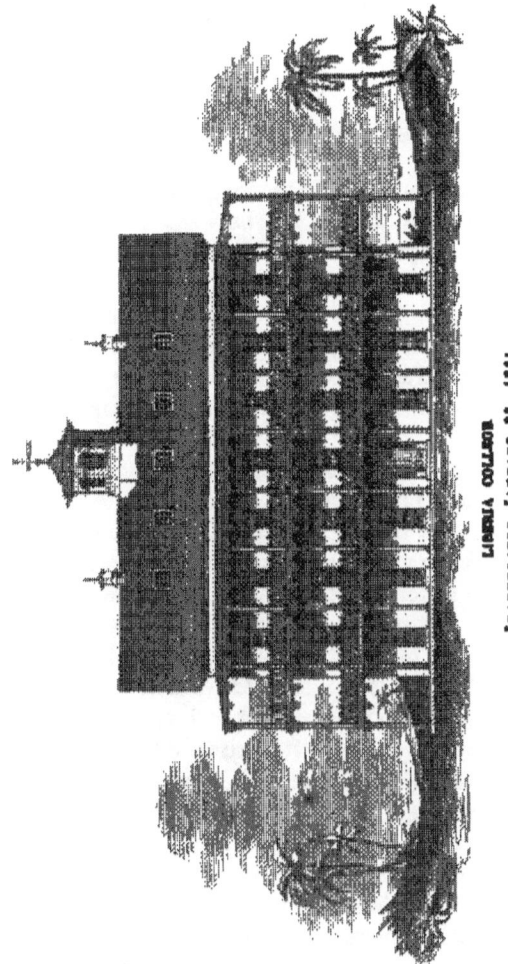

LIBERIA COLLEGE.
INAUGURATED JANUARY 23, 1862.

HOPE FOR AFRICA.

"ETHIOPIA shall soon stretch out her hands unto God."—PSALM 68 : 31.

THE continent of Africa occupies an important geographical position. It lies between two great oceans—the highways of the principal portions of commerce. It contains twelve millions of square miles, with a population of one hundred and sixty millions. But, notwithstanding its physical and relative importance, it has lain, until a comparatively recent period, shrouded from the view of the inhabitants of other portions of the earth.

While the spirit of adventure has opened up the most uninviting parts of Europe; while Asia, with its impenetrable jungle and ferocious animals, has been traversed from one end to the other; while the ancient and mighty forests of America have fallen before the power of enterprise and the charm of civilization—the highest peak of the Rocky Mountains scaled, the Andes and the Cordilleras measured; while the distant isles of the sea have been visited and occupied by intelligence, industry, and enterprise; while the cold and barren, and almost inaccessible regions of the earth have been approached and explored as far as human beings are found—Africa, lying in the very pathway of commerce, offering as many inducements to the seekers after scientific knowledge as any other land, presenting as numerous objects for the labors of the philanthropist as any other country, has been passed by by the traveler and the philanthropist, and the civilized world has been left to entertain at best but the most vague and unsatisfactory conjectures as to the character of the country, and the condition of its inhabitants.

To the majority of civilized and enlightened men, Africa is hardly ever made a subject of earnest thought. Various interests of more immediate concern crowd out thoughts of a land which is spoken of, perhaps, only when instances of degradation, ignorance, and superstition are referred to. The other portion of the civilized world, who think and speak of Africa, are divided in their views and feelings with regard to that land, and in the motives which actuate them to be at all interested. Some regard it as a place with which a lucrative trade may be "driven;" where the articles of commerce, palm-oil, cam-wood, ivory, and other rare productions may be obtained. These speak of Africa only in connection with these things. All their interests in the land are of a commercial nature. Others, with souls more sordid and hearts more avaricious, who are never once troubled by any sentiment of humanity, are interested in Africa only as a scene for plunder and carnage. From these, Africa has had the most frequent and the most constant visits, during the last three centuries. They have spread all along the coast of that peninsula—formerly the abode of peace and plenty, of industry and love—"arrows, firebrands, and death." In their pursuit of blood—"not beasts' but human gore"—they have scattered desolation, and misery, and degradation into all parts of the land whither they have had access; so that not unfrequently has it occurred that some unfortunate and lonely sufferer, standing amid a scene of desolation, having escaped the cruel chase of the slaver, whose ruthless hands have borne away his relatives and acquaintances, has earnestly cursed civilization, and has solemnly prayed, as he has stood surveying the melancholy relics of his home, that an insurmountable and impenetrable barrier—some wall of mountain height—might be erected between his country and all civilized nations.

Only a few, very few, have regarded Africa as a land inhabited by human beings, children of the same common Father, travelers to the same judgment-seat of Christ, and heirs of the same awful immortality. These few have endeavored to hold up that land as the object of the sympathy, the labors, and the prayers of the Christian world. They have held her up as the victim of unfortunate circumstances, which have operated against her progress, and prevented her from keeping pace, in the march of human improvement, with other and more favored portions of the earth. These few have endeavored, and are now endeavoring to awaken a deeper interest in that land. Through their noble efforts, that forgotten country is becoming better known. Its inhabitants are receiving more of the sympathy of the enlightened portion of mankind; and efforts are making to introduce among them the blessings of civilization and Christianity—to accelerate the day when "Ethiopia shall stretch out her hands unto God."

But there are adversaries. There are those who have no sympathy to bestow upon the African. His complexion and hair furnish to them conclusive reasons why he should be excluded from their benevolence. They wish nothing to do with him. Their charities, when the negro is mentioned, immediately contract. Their

Christian love is ample enough to embrace all Europe, and other countries inhabited by the Caucasian, but it can go no further. Upon other branches of the human family they look down with arrogance and contempt. And such persons may be found in enlightened countries, professing Christianity, and priding themselves on their civilization and culture. But do not such feelings prove them to be connected rather closely with those remote ages when the extent of one's clan or tribe or district formed the limit of all his benevolent operations? Does not their conduct constantly remind those who meet them of their intimate relations with the barbarous past? Are they not sadly deficient of that magnanimous and noble liberality which Christianity seeks to inspire, when it declares that of "one blood God hath made *all the nations* of the earth"?

There are others, who believe, or affect to believe, that this people are doomed to degradation and servitude; that the malediction uttered by Noah—evidently against the descendants of Canaan, and which has long since received its fulfillment—follows the African race; and that therefore all efforts to elevate them will be unavailing. Yet some of these persons profess to believe in the regenerating and elevating power of the Gospel. They will declaim long and loudly, upon the efficiency of Christianity to redeem and dignify man—to spread, wherever it goes, light and liberty, and the blessings of an exalted civilization. But, in their minds, Africa seems to form an exception. The promises in the Bible of the universal prevalence of righteousness and truth, are not far-reaching enough to affect her case. The ignorance, degradation, and misery of the land are so deep and revolting, as to baffle the recuperative power of the Gospel.

But the Lord, whose ways are not as our ways, and whose thoughts are not as our thoughts, has declared that the earth shall be filled with his knowledge, as the waters cover the sea. Glorious truth! The salvation which Christ has purchased for us is a "common salvation." It is confined neither to countries nor races. It knows no limits. All complexions, all classes and conditions are equally within the sphere of its operation. "Go ye into all the world," said the Divine Author of the salvation, "and preach the Gospel to *every* creature." Its applicability is universal. All the accessible dominions of the world may be blessed by it. It will rectify all disorder, banish every vice, loose every bond, and having eradicated the causes of all the sins and sorrows and sufferings of the human family, it will spread righteousness and truth, harmony and peace, liberty and love, over the whole face of this sin-stricken globe. These are the glorious and wide-spread results which Christianity promises to achieve. And who will dare to say that Africa will not participate in these general blessings? Who will dare to affirm that Africa will remain in her gloom, when the glory of the Lord shall have filled the whole earth?

But if these promises be considered too general, there are passages in the word of God, there are promises and types which have special reference to Africa. "Behold Philistia and Tyre, with Ethiopia; this man was born there. The labor of Egypt, and merchandise of Ethiopia and of the Sabeans, men of stature, shall come over unto thee, and they shall be thine." And the words of the text: "Princes shall come out of Egypt. Ethiopia shall soon stretch out her hands unto God." No one that remembers the reference in the Scripture to the skin of the Ethiopian, will doubt that these prophecies belong to the negro. We see the eunuch of Candace, queen of the Ethiopians, going on his way rejoicing, because believing in Jesus; and we seem to have a pledge of Africa's evangelization. When the wicked Herod was plotting the murder of the infant Redeemer of mankind, an angel appeared to Joseph in a dream, and said, "Arise, and take the young child and his mother, and flee into the land of Egypt"—*into the land of Egypt*, IN AFRICA. Africa, in the providence of God, according to the declarations of prophecy, was the land chosen to shelter the Saviour of the world. If, in the hour of his danger, Africa was the chosen asylum from the cruelty of his royal enemy; if, in the hour of his affliction, he sought a refuge in that land, will he not now, in the day of *her* trial and *her* affliction, remember her? Was not his flight to, and sojourn in that land, a token of his favor? Driven from Asia, the land of his birth, from among his own people, that land, now down-trodden, gave him welcome. And if it be true that to as many as received him, he gave power to become the sons of God, may not Africa, though she did not then receive him in that higher and more spiritual sense, expect to share in the privilege of becoming a child of God? Will he not yet, in his might, as King of kings, and Lord of lords, gird on his sword, and ride through that land, conquering and to conquer? Will he not overturn, as he is already beginning to do, and overturn and overturn, until he establish his kingdom there? Yes; we take it, that as he suffered in Africa, in the days of his humiliation, he will yet reign in that land in his glory.

But there is an ampler prophecy still—a more express type: "Let us go," to quote the language of Mr. Melvill, " and look on the Redeemer as he toils towards

Calvary. Who is it that, in the ordering of Providence, has been appointed to carry his cross? A Cyrenian, an African. As Africa had something to do with his earlier days, so she has to do with his final hours. 'And as they came out, they found a man of Cyrene, Simon by name: him they compelled to bear his cross.' We read the prophecy; we apprehend the type. Not without meaning was one of the sons of Africa selected to bear the cross after Christ, and thus to fill a post to which the martyrs and confessors of every age of Christianity have counted it their highest honor to succeed. It was as though to tell us that even Africa shall yet be brought to the discipleship of Jesus. Europe gave not this type of the Gentile world submitting to Christ. Asia was not permitted to own the favored individual. America, as yet unknown to the rest of the earth, might not send the representative of heathenism. Africa is the privileged country; an African follows Jesus. Oh! the darkness of many generations seems scattered; and I rejoice in the assurance that the land of slaves shall be the home of freedom, the land of misery the home of happiness, the land of idolatry the home of Christianity."*

Some have been inclined to regard Africa as a doomed land, on account of the protracted night which has hung over it. Empires have arisen and fallen; the arts and sciences have been born, fostered, grown up to strength and maturity in other lands, while Africa remains in its primitive simplicity and barbarism, contributing nothing to the well-being of mankind. From this fact, it has been argued that there is a natural and invincible incapacity for improvement in the race, forbidding all hope of their ever becoming a power in the

* Melvill's Sermons, vol. II. 1850.

world. This were a correct inference, if it could be shown that Africans have had equal facilities for improvement with those races which have made such rapid strides in civilization, or if it could be shown that any people precisely in their circumstances have made any marked advancement. The negro has been inhabiting a country by whose physical peculiarities he has been deprived of the intercourse of the civilized and enlightened world.

This land, for wise purposes doubtless, is rendered inaccessible to foreigners, by fevers produced by the exhalations arising from the marshy alluvial lands, which border all the intertropical regions; it has, therefore, been shut out for the most part, from the means of improvement. Men talk selfishly and scornfully of the long-continued barbarism and degradation of Africa, as if civilization were indigenous to any country; as if the soil and climate of some countries could give existence, and vitality, and growth to the arts and sciences. If this were the case, we should despair of Africa's ever rising from her abject condition. But all the teachings of general and particular history, all individual and national experience are opposed to such an idea. No nation has ever been found, which, by its own unaided efforts, by some powerful inward impulse, has arisen from barbarism and degradation to civilization and respectability. It is very true that the circumstances of some nations or communities have been more favorable than those of others, for receiving and retaining and improving upon the elements of civilization. But there is nothing in race or blood, in color or hair, that imparts susceptibility of improvement to one people over another. Knowledge, which lies at the basis of all human progress, came from heaven. It must be acquired; it is not innate. The mind left to itself from infancy, without the means of culture, remains, if not blank, yet destitute of all those ideas which constitute a man civilized. If it be strong and vigorous, it will, instead of rising in the scale of virtue and civilization, make deeper and more awful plunges into barbarism. The richness of the uncultivated soil shows itself in the rankness and luxuriance of the weeds which it produces. The soil, then, must be cultivated, if we expect to reap a harvest of any value. So with the mind. The intellectual plow and rake must be used, and the good seed introduced. Knowledge must be imparted. As one man learns it from another, so nation learns it from nation. Civilization is handed from one people to another, its great fountain and source being the great God of the universe.

Those nations that are foremost in civilization and science were once in abject degradation. No one in the days of Cæsar or Tacitus could ever have predicted that the barbarism and savage wildness of the Germans would give place to the learning, refinement, and culture which that people now exhibit. When Cicero pronounced the Britons unfit for slaves, on account of their stupidity, who would have ventured to affirm, without appearing to insult the understanding of men, that that people would become one of the leading powers of the earth ? "Nothing," says Mr. Macaulay, "in the early existence of Britain, indicated the greatness which she was destined to attain." Now, I would ask, if it be true that there is innate ability in certain races to rise in the scale of civilization; and if that ability, as some would intimate, exists in those which have already risen, why did the Britons, when Greece and Rome flourished in all their grandeur, remain insignificant and unknown? Why was not that self-civilizing power exhibited by them, which many now look for in the Africans? Nor are Africans the only people that have remained stationary in these latter days of multiplied facilities for improvement. There are many tribes in whose veins courses the renowned Caucasian blood, sunk to-day in a degradation as deep, and in an ignorance as profound as any tribe in Africa. If civilization is inborn in the Caucasian, as some affirm; if it is indigenous to all the countries which he inhabits, why are the tribes to which we have referred, no further advanced? Ought not every land which Caucasians inhabit, to be in a high state of civilization? But many are far from such a state. Look at the regions of Siberia, of Lapland. Look at the peasantry of many of the countries of Europe. Why are they so far down in the scale of civilization? And look at those countries in the south of Europe, Turkey, Greece, Italy, Spain, and Portugal, which formerly flourished, and contained within themselves all the learning and wisdom that existed in the world. They have sadly degenerated. They are comparatively insignificant. Why did not their Caucasian nature, if it did not urge them onward to higher attainments, keep them in the same leading positions among the nations? The answer is at hand. Their natures remain the same. Their soil and climate are the same. Demosthenes and Cicero, Alexander and Cæsar, saw no serener sky, they felt no more genial breezes than their degenerate posterity. The sun shines with the same power and glory; the moon moves on with the same soft and silvery sweetness; the stars are as beautiful and bright as when Homer and Virgil felt their inspiration. What, then, causes the difference? *The moral circum-*

stances of the people are changed. The circumstances that have surrounded them for several centuries have been of a character to retard their progress.

Men, are to a certain extent, the creatures of the circumstances in which they live. Very often, what they achieve depends less upon their personal qualities than upon surrounding influences. The African forms no exception to this rule. Between him and other men there is not that difference which some have labored to establish. There is, indeed, no essential difference between any two men. Men, however, have drawn formidable lines of separation between themselves and others, who, happening not to have been blessed with the same propitious circumstances, have not risen to the same intellectual or social standing. How true the words of the poet!—

> "Alas! what differs more than man from man?
> And whence this difference? Whence but from himself?
> For see the universal race endowed
> With the same upright form."*

The African, then, is in the rear of the European, not because of any essential difference existing in their nature, but only on account of differing circumstances. In consequence of various influences to which I have already adverted, rendering the coast of his native land unhealthy to foreigners, civilization and Christianity, with their concomitant blessings, have not been generally introduced.

Until very recently, the country was not known beyond its maritime frontiers. And in keeping with the general disposition to exaggerate the good or evil qualities of what is unknown, various stories were put in circulation with regard to this land — stories which had

* Wordsworth.

the effect to beget indifference on the part of some, and actual dread of penetrating the country on the part of others. Some of these stories of wonders in the interior, and frightful appearances on the coast, arose in remote antiquity, and are to this day current among the ignorant. Recent explorations show that many of those horrible things had no reality but in the prejudices of their inventors. Perhaps the most ancient and most amusing stories told of this land, are those by Hanno, the Carthaginian commander, who went on a voyage of colonization and discovery along the Atlantic coast, about five hundred years before the Christian era. He says in his report: "We passed a country burning with fires and perfumes, and streams of fire supplied from it fell into the sea. The country was impassable on account of the heat. We sailed quickly thence, being much terrified; and passing on for four days, we discovered at night a country full of fire. In the middle was a lofty fire larger than the rest, which seemed to touch the stars." This surpasses even those terrible pictures which children, in their florid imaginations, are accustomed to draw of that land.

All these stories of the physical character of the country, blended with exaggerated statements of the moral degradation of its inhabitants, have tended to keep away enterprise and civilization from Africa. Men have been willing barely to tolerate a trade with the outskirts of the country; and they would not even do this, were it not for the lucrativeness of the trade. And it has been the policy of African traders, though they know that many of the tales in circulation about Africa are devoid of foundation, to assist in giving them currency, in order to keep away competition. Can any wonder, in view of these circumstances, that

Africa still lags behind in the march of human improvement?

And when, with these things, we take into consideration the regular and thoroughly organized efforts which have been put forth to keep back the African; when we think of the numerous obstacles which have been thrown into the way of his advancement by the avarice and wickedness of men, do we not rather wonder that he is no lower down in barbarism? Do we not rather wonder that any portion of this people should have made progress in civilization, in literature, and in science?

Shall we here tell you of the sufferings which the slave-trade has entailed upon them? Shall we tell you of their sorrows in the countries of their captivity? Oh! we would not harrow up the feelings of this audience with tales of woe. We would but refer to slavery and the slave-trade. Those names alone are sufficient to call up emotions of sympathy wherever there exist the feelings of humanity. The wrongs of the African fill the darkest page of human history. To recount the barbarities which the Christian nations of Europe and of America have inflicted, and are now inflicting upon the negro, "would fill volumes, and they should be written with tears instead of ink, and on sack-cloth instead of parchment." We refer not merely to those physical annoyances, and diabolical tortures, and debasing usages, to which, in the countries of their exile, they have been subjected, but also to those deeper wrongs whose tendency has been to dwarf the soul, to emasculate the mind. You have perhaps read the narrative of African sufferings; but painfully intense as they are, they are only the outside—they are only the visible. There are a thousand little evils which can never be expressed. There is a sorrow of the heart, with which the stranger can not intermeddle. There are secret agonies known only to God, which are far more acute than any external tortures. Oh! it is not the smiting of the back, until the earth is crimsoned with streams of·blood; it is not the pursuing of human beings with blood-hounds; it is not the amputation of the limbs; it is not even the killing of the body; it is not these that are the keenest sufferings that a people can undergo. Oh! no; these affect only the outward man, and may leave untouched the majestic mind. But those inflictions which tend to contract and destroy the mind; those cruelties which benumb the sensibility of the soul, those influences which chill and arrest the currency of the heart's affections—these are the awful instruments of real suffering and degradation; and these have been made to operate upon the African.

But mark the providence of God in the case of this people. The very means which, to all human appearance, seemed calculated to crush them out from the earth, have been converted into means of blessing. In the countries of their exile, they have come under the influences of Christianity, from which they were debarred in their own country, by physical circumstances. They have been almost miraculously preserved. It may be said of them as of the Israelites in Egypt: "The more they afflicted them, the more they multiplied and grew." They have grown despite affliction, both numerically and intellectually; their national life has been remarkably intense; they still retain in undiminished vigor their integrity as a people.

And, as if in fulfillment of a Divine plan, some are beginning to return to their fatherland from the house of their bitter pilgrimage, laden with the blessings of Christianity and civilization, and are successfully introducing them among their benighted brethren. Liberia, the region of Africa which these pioneers inhabit, insignificant though it may be among the nations of the earth, is an important spot on that continent. It is a center whence is beginning to radiate to different points of that land the light of Christianity. There are fifteen thousand civilized and Christianized Africans striving to accomplish the twofold work of establishing and maintaining an independent nationality, and of introducing the Gospel among untold millions of unevangelized and barbarous men. Their residence on that coast of only thirty years has already brought to pass important and salutary revolutions in the condition of that portion of Africa.

Liberia has resisted the influence of heathenism. She has stood her ground against the encroachments of a superstition which, considering the general character of her citizens, she was but little prepared to meet. She has completely, in all her feebleness, annihilated the slave-trade along seven hundred miles of coast. Before the establishment of that little Republic, the tribes in all the extent of country now within our jurisdiction, and under our influence, were perpetually harassed by the incursions of those monsters in human form, the slave-traders. They could feel secure at no time. War! war! war! and carnage were continually the cry, and every nook and corner was made to tremble. Young and old, male and female, fell victims to the heartless marauders. Those who escaped did so only by fleeing from the neighborhood of the slave-hunters to the thickets and swamps—to the milder and safer neighborhood of leopards and boa constrictors.

But, blessed be God, a different state of things now exists.

When, forty years ago, the small band of eighty colored persons settled on Cape Mesurado, far away, near five thousand miles across the sea from the place of their birth, in a strange and insalubrious climate, surrounded by hostile tribes and other unpropitious influences, owning only a few acres of land, no one would have supposed that in less than forty years, in the lifetime of some of the first settlers, that people would so enlarge and spread themselves, so extend their influences as to possess over fifty thousand square miles of territory, holding under their jurisdiction over two hundred thousand souls. Tribes which, when they first landed on those shores, could easily have overwhelmed them and swept them into the sea, they now compel to cease intercourse with the slave-trader, to forget their mutual feuds in obedience to Christian law, and to cease from wars and bloodshed. They induce them, instead of the sword, to use the plowshare, and instead of the spear, the pruning-hook. And this influence is growing. Liberia is known and respected for hundreds of miles in the interior; and by the contact which is every day occurring between traders and transient visitors from the far interior and the civilized Liberians, our influence is going out in all directions, and a great work is being accomplished in this part of Africa.

But you may ask for positive advancement in the Republic of Liberia. You may point me to the progress of this country; you may point me to the physical revolutions which Anglo-Saxon genius has produced over all this land; you may bid me look at the various appliances of civilization, and you may ask: Can Liberia show any thing like these?

In reply, I might point you to numerous physical changes in Liberia. I might point you to numerous instances of decided improvement in the physical aspect of that portion of Africa. But I now choose to refer you to the moral work that has been accomplished. I point you to barbarism encroached upon and overcome; to carnage and bloodshed arrested; to peace produced among belligerents; to confidence and security, comfort and happiness restored; to lawful traffic taking the place of unlawful; and I ask whether the triumphs of love over hatred; the triumphs of peace over war; the triumphs of humanity over barbarism and outrage; the triumphs of Christianity over heathenism, be not entitled to at least as much respect as the triumph of physical agencies over the face of nature? I do not know of any other place in the world where fifteen thousand persons are doing so important a work as those fifteen thousand Liberians. Oh! that they may have the wisdom to comprehend the responsibility of their position, and the grace to discharge the duties it involves!

The land is gradually opening. The portals which have been kept closed through all the historic ages by the repulsive inhospitality of nature, are yielding to the enterprise, the greed of trade, and the missionary zeal of the nineteenth century. Barth in the east and north, Livingstone in the south, have brought before the world treasures of information with regard to that land. Seymour and Sims,[*] citizens of Liberia, on the west have rendered valuable service. Explorations in various sections of the country are now going on. From almost every point of the compass expeditions are proceeding to the interior of the continent. Soon

---

[*] The last two are names but little known, but not undeserving of mention, if adventure, and endurance, and suffering for the sake of enlarging the sphere of human knowledge, entitle any to be numbered among the benefactors of mankind.

the mysteries of the land will be unfolded to the gaze and contemplation of an astonished world. These are the preliminaries to that great event which is predicted in the text: "Ethiopia shall soon stretch forth her hands unto God."

We have endeavored carefully to examine this glorious and oft-cited passage in the original Hebrew; and it has occurred to us that the passage might have been literally rendered: "Ethiopia shall *suddenly* stretch out her hands unto God." The idea contained in the verb *tarits*, rendered, "*shall soon stretch out*," does not seem to refer so much to the *time* as to the *manner* of the action predicted. The first meaning of the verb is *to run;* so it is rendered in Psalm 119:32, "I will *run* in the way of thy commandments;" and in Jeremiah 23:31, "I have not sent these prophets, yet they *ran*," etc. In the Hiphil form, the form which occurs in the text, the verb means to *cause to run;* or to lead on hastily, to do a thing quickly before the occurrence of any obstacle; hence, *suddenly.* Gesenius, the distinguished German philologist, translates the passage: Ethiopia shall let her hands make haste to God."

If, then, the idea is, that Ethiopia shall *suddenly* be redeemed, is there not furnished a rebuke to those who, because Africa has lain so long in darkness and gloom, and because of the unpromising aspect of her present moral condition, give themselves up to despair, and fancy that there will never be the inauguration of better times? Why should men at any time venture unqualified opinions on matters in which the intellectual vision is necessarily bounded, and with regard to which experience so abundantly shows they can not arrive at conclusions altogether free from error, however extensive the induction upon which they base their reasonings? The problem of African disenthrallment and elevation is beyond the power of human ingenuity to solve. Nothing short of Omniscience could so lay down the premises for reasoning upon this important subject, as to secure a result entirely free from error. Can the most acute and far-reaching mind indicate the antecedents and concomitants of that remarkable period when a nation shall be born in a day? We may now be upon the very eve of events which are to usher in the redemption of Africa. The time, yea, the set time to favor Africa may be just about to break upon us in all its glory. And it may be that centuries form the interval which lies between us and the desired consummation. We can not tell; though from the signs of the times we feel justified in taking a hopeful rather than a desponding view.

The success which has already attended the efforts to civilize and Christianize that dark land gives encouraging promise of a glorious future.

"Within the last twenty-five years more than one hundred Christian churches have been organized in that country, and upwards of fifteen thousand hopeful converts have been gathered into those churches. Nearly two hundred schools are in full operation in connection with these various missions, and not less than sixteen thousand native youths are receiving a Christian training in those schools at the present moment. More than twenty different dialects have been studied out and reduced to writing, into many of which large portions of sacred Scripture, as well as other religious books, have been translated, printed, and circulated among the people; and we are, no doubt, in the bounds of truth and probability, when it is assumed that some knowledge of the Christian salvation has been brought by direct and indirect means within the reach of at least five millions of immortal beings, who had never before heard of the blessed name of the Saviour.

"Bright Christian lights now begin to blaze up at intervals, along a line of sea-coast of more than three thousand miles, where unbroken night formerly reigned. The everlasting Gospel is now preached in Kumasi and Abomi, the capitals respectively of Ashantee and Dahomey, two of the most barbarous kingdoms on the face of the earth. Christian missions are now being established all over the kingdom of Yoruba, a land once wholly given up to the slave-trade and bloodshed. Along the banks of the far interior Niger, where the bones of the great African traveler have slumbered for half a century, Christian lights are springing up in the track of the exploring expedition. At Old Calabar, a place renowned in former times not only for being one of the chief seats of the foreign slave-trade, but for the unparalleled cruelties and barbarities of its people, the Gospel is not only preached, but the Spirit of God is poured out upon that debased people. The Gospel has recently been proclaimed by our own (Presbyterian) missionaries from Corisco, on the hights of the Sierra del Crystal Mountains, to a people who had not only never before heard it, but who themselves were unknown to the Christian world until within a few years past. When all these things are taken into consideration, every discerning mind must see at once that a footing of immense advantage has already been acquired; and if present measures, with such modifications as may be suggested by experience, are followed up, in dependence upon Divine aid, the time is not far distant when the light of the Gospel shall reach the darkest and most remote corner of that great continent."*

There is a strong probability that the progress of truth in Africa will be rapid and sudden. The missionary does not encounter there, as in Asia, any formidable superstition to be battered down. Though the people acknowledge the existence of good and bad spirits, they have no system of religion protected by the sanction of a hoary antiquity; so that the work of evangelization need not be commenced by the slow process of undermining ancient and venerable systems of belief. The missionary's hardest work is to check the downward currency of the affections, to beget thoughtfulness on the subject of religion, to instill ideas of religion into the mind. His work is more constructive than destructive. He has nothing to demolish; he has only to arrange his materials, and proceed to build.

We look for great things in Africa during the next five-and-twenty years. Why should it be thought a thing impossible for that moral desert to bloom and blossom as the rose? Why should it be regarded as

* *Princeton Review*, July, 1858.

impossible for the moral night which has so long rested upon that land to give place to a glorious day? If the Lord has declared that Ethiopia shall *suddenly* stretch forth her hands unto God, why should we be inclined to limit him in his power? Is there any thing too hard for the Lord? If he be Almighty, if he can create at all, if he can bring a single atom of matter from the abyss of nothingness into existence, then what can he not do? He only speaks, and it is done; he commands, and it stands fast; he spake, and the confusion of chaos was hushed, and the world—the beautiful cosmos—came forth with all its symmetry and grandeur. Then why should there be any thing impossible in the doctrine that Ethiopia—benighted and outraged Ethiopia—shall *suddenly* stretch out her hands unto God? Why should it be thought impossible for him to bring order out of the moral and intellectual chaos of that land?

If the men who are skeptical as to the rapid evangelization and civilization of Africa could only catch the hum of the missionary schools scattered in various portions of that land; could they only hear the earnest appeals of leading men among various tribes for Christianity and its teachings; could they hear, as we hear, who live on that barbarous coast, the murmurings of the fountains of the great deep of ignorance and superstition, which are breaking up all around us; could they hear the noise, which we hear, of the rattling of dry bones strewed over that immense valley, they would cease to doubt; they would recognize, as we do, the promising future before us; they would see that a day of life and joy is rapidly dawning upon Africa, and that there is a strong probability that He whose right it is to reign will suddenly come and take possession of that land. It need not imply any pretension to prophetic insight for us to declare that we live in the shadows of remarkable events in the history of Africa — events whose consequences will be of transcendent importance and unending interest, not only to that down-trodden land, but to the whole human race. Oh! that the Christian Church throughout the world would be fervent in prayer and diligent in labor, that the day may be hastened when "Ethiopia shall stretch forth her hands unto God!"

Have the black men of the United States no part to take in this work? There lies the land of your fathers, in its natural beauty and glory — a country well-watered every where as the garden of the Lord — a country of hills and valleys, of rivers and brooks, of fields and plains.

"Every prospect pleases
And only man is vile."

There it lies also in its spiritual desolation — millions of your brethren in the most awful destitution. Have you, O ye children of Africa! no tear to shed, no sympathy to bestow, no effort to put forth for your gray-haired parent in sorrow and affliction; for your brethren who have not, as you have, enjoyed the blessings of civilization and Christianity? Are you ashamed of Africa because she has been plundered and rifled by wicked men? Do you turn your backs upon your mother because she is not high among the nations? Are you neglecting her with the hope of elevating yourselves in this country? Oh! remember that Europeans can not carry on the work so much needed in that land, and which experience proves that you are so well fitted to achieve. This all-important work is yours. White men go there; they wither and die. You were brought away by the permission of Providence, doubtless, that you might be prepared and fitted to return and instruct your brethren. If you turn away from the work to which Providence evidently calls you, with the selfish hope of elevating yourselves in this country, beware lest the calamities come upon you which are threatened to those who neglect to honor their parents. I give it as my most serious conviction, that there will be no real prosperity among the Africans in this land, no proper respect shown them by the dominant race, so long as they persist, as a mass, in ignoring the claims of Africa upon them. All their efforts at self-elevation here which shall leave Africa out of the question, will be as "sowing to the wind."

It is gratifying to find, however, that there has been, during the last few years, a decided change for the better in the feelings of many toward Africa. Formerly, those who rose up among the colored people of this country to plead for African civilization by her own descendants, were denounced as traitors, and were often in danger of being stoned as enemies to the peace and prosperity of their brethren. But now some of the leading men among you are taking large views of duty, and no longer consider it a mark of weakness to plead for the evangelization of millions of souls by their brethren in this land. They no longer consider it disgraceful to urge colored men of intelligence and enterprise to turn their attention to Africa.

It has pleased Almighty God, in late years, as I have endeavored to show, to make interesting openings for the introduction of the Gospel into that land. Scores of doors which, a few years ago, were strongly bolted, are now, by the Divine agency, thrown open before the Church. Broad entrances are proffered the Gospel of Christ. Will not black men who have so freely received, hasten to give the waters of life to the perishing millions? A call is to-day made upon you from your benighted brethren. Are you prepared to spurn it? Have you no response for this Macedonian call? I entreat you, by all the blessings you *have* enjoyed, by all the blessings you now enjoy, by all the blessings you hope to enjoy, remember Africa. I beseech you by the dire necessities of our people; by their long night of sorrow and suffering; by the cries louder than thunder, that are wafted from the far interior, upon every wind that blows; by the encouraging prospects before us; by all the promises of God—men and brethren, come over and help us—help "Ethiopia to stretch forth her hands unto God."

A VINDICATION OF THE AFRICAN RACE;

BEING A

BRIEF EXAMINATION OF THE ARGUMENTS

IN FAVOR OF

AFRICAN INFERIORITY.

(First published in Liberia in August, 1857.)

"Mislike me not for my complexion,
   The shadowed livery of the burnished sun,
   To whom I am a neighbor, and near bred;
   Bring me the fairest creature northern born,
   Where Phœbus' fire scarce thaws the icicles,
   And let us make incisions . . .
   To prove whose blood is reddest, his or mine."
                                           —SHAKESPEARE.

"Alas! what differs more than man from man?
   And whence that difference? whence but from himself?
   For see the universal Race endowed
   With the same upright form."
                                           —WORDSWORTH.

NOAH'S MALEDICTION.*

"Opinionum commenta dies delet, naturæ judicia confirmat."

THE African race, in consequence of its peculiar physical characteristics, and the circumstances unfavorable to its progress in human improvement, by which, for more than two thousand years, it has been surrounded, has been generally and variously misrepresented and traduced. For centuries, has this race engaged the attention of the enlightened and scientific among other races. Its complexion and hair have furnished difficult ethnological problems; and the fact that it has for a long time stood at the very bottom of civilization, and has seemed to be in the rear of every other people, subjected in its own land, and in all other lands, to the most degrading oppression, has suggested to some the idea, that it is naturally and irrecoverably, an inferior race, and that some secret and inevitable, though inexplicable, influence operates upon it.

Various theories have been started as furnishing satisfactory explanation of the causes operating upon this unfortunate race. Of these, none has been more strenuously urged by the opposers of the race than that which refers its condition to a malediction recorded in Genesis 9 : 25, 26, 27. They who support this theory take the ground that the curse was denounced against Ham, the progenitor of the African race, and all his posterity;

* Genesis 9 : 25, 26, 27.

affirming that the general condition, character and capabilities of Africans point them out as the subjects of the malediction. Thus, by an argument *à posteriori*, notwithstanding the reading of the passage and other circumstances plainly indicate that the curse was uttered against Canaan, the youngest son of Ham, they infer that it was uttered against Ham and all his posterity, simply because, on other grounds they can not, or will not, account for the condition of the African race. They prove the *application* of the curse from the condition of the race, and then argue the *necessity* of that condition from the application of the curse. Does not such reasoning marvelously involve what logicians call the *argumentum in orbem ?*

Before proceeding to notice the justness of that interpretation of Noah's malediction, which refers it to the African race, it may be proper to remark, that such an interpretation of that passage of Scripture was not insisted upon until the commencement of the unhallowed traffic in African slaves; in which traffic, at its beginning, nearly all the nations of Christendom participated. The more conscientious among those who engaged in the trade, not being able to divest themselves of responsibility in thus robbing of their rights beings, whose claims to humanity they could not disprove, "wrested" this passage of Scripture in justification of their proceedings; affirming that the race was doomed to slavery, and that themselves were only *instruments* in verifying the prediction of its doom. The Church, also, countenanced these unjust proceedings, by giving the weight of its sanction to the erroneous, but designing construction put upon that passage of the word of God; a passage evidently recorded to encourage and justify the Israelites in their invasion of the land of

Canaan, and destruction of the Canaanites — a people, whom their own iniquities, and those of their ancestors, had rendered fit vessels of the wrath and righteous retribution of heaven. When we say that the Church countenanced these proceedings, we do not mean that it did this *of design*, or with any view of deriving gain from the avarice of slave-traders. It being no doubt the prevalent opinion of the times, influential organs of the Church, not regarding it as any point of importance, requiring more extensive investigations, coincided with the popular view, that they might not, by insisting upon a point of apparently minor importance, offend the prejudices of the multitude and thus injure their influence.* Men, whose characters were otherwise irreproachable, were induced by the habits of thought then prevailing, and by the supposed convenience of slave labor, to purchase the African captives brought to their shores. Some even of the most eminent divines were so far implicated in the error, that they, with perfect ease of conscience, held negroes in bondage. The distinguished William Penn, Rev. George Whitefield, of world-wide celebrity, President Edwards, author of several standard works in Theology, were *slaveholders*. But this "minor" point grew to such magnitude, and in its influence was so injurious, that both clergymen and laymen came forward and opposed the enslavement of Africans, as "contrary to the laws of God, and as outraging every principle of justice recognized among men;" insisting that "God hath made of one blood all the nations of the earth;" and that if the Gospel were

---

* There are some in the Church who believe it right to accommodate the teachings of the Bible to the opinions and circumstances of men, when such accommodation does not involve a palpable violation of any clearly revealed principle; while others maintain that the "whole counsel of God," both expressed and implied, should be "declared," independently of the prejudices and opinions of men.

3

universally and rightly appealed to, no other bond would be known among men, but that of Christian brotherhood."

But the common interpretation of the curse under consideration is still extant among some divines, particularly in America, and is used by them to justify that system of enormous iniquity, which of certain sections of that country is denominated the "peculiar institution." They contend that it is fruitless to endeavor to elevate the African; for he is doomed to perpetual servitude, and is, therefore, fitted for no other condition.* Hence, one of them did not hesitate to affirm that he felt a conscientious reluctance to offer a single prayer, if by that prayer all the slaves in the Union would be set free.

It does not, however, admit of dispute, that the authority of divines of acknowledged ability, on either side of the question, is not to be despised; and it is rather a dangerous thing for a mere neophyte, hardly yet from the schools, to differ where learned and venerable doctors agree. But the question as to the true application of the curse must, after all, be decided, not by authority, but by the weight of argument in support of the positions assumed. Therefore, while yielding what

---

* Being in the city of New-York on the Thanksgiving Day of 1850, we were invited by Rev. J. B. Pinney to attend divine services at one of the most popular and influential churches in that city. The pastor, a D.D. of eminent learning and ability, preached a political discourse having reference to the Fugitive Slave Law, then recently enacted. In the course of his sermon, which was in justification of the law, the minister took a view of the condition and character of the colored people in the United States, in which he made an assertion to the effect, that the efforts of those who were endeavoring to elevate Africans in America were, and always would be, fruitless. "The decree," he remarked, "has gone forth, and we can not reverse it." "Cursed be Canaan, a servant of servants shall he be unto his brethren." That was the first of our hearing such weight given to this interpretation and application of Noah's malediction; and though not over eighteen years old, we experienced, as it were, an intuitive revulsion of mind never to be forgotten.

we conceive to be a reasonable submission to authority, we venture to differ most decidedly from the "doctors." But in differing from them, we are prepared to make proper allowance. They have doubtless been "brought up to their opinions" upon this subject; and, regarding the whole matter as of inconsiderable importance, they do not exert themselves to make further investigations in reference to it. It is a fact that when men maintain views inherited from their ancestors, and which accord with their inclinations, they never allow the possibility of their being wrong to trouble them; and they care not to inquire into the grounds of such views, lest such inquiry lead to a detection of their error, and consequent mortification of their pride. They love their opinions, of whatever nature they are, and they cleave to them, acting on the principle: "My opinions, may they always be right; but my opinions, right or wrong."

But let us see from the reading of Genesis 9 : 25, 26, 27, and from certain historical circumstances, whether that is a fair interpretation which applies that prophecy to the African race:

"And Noah awoke from his wine, and knew what his younger son had done unto him. And he said: 'Cursed be Canaan; a servant of servants shall he be unto his brethren.' And he said: 'Blessed be the Lord God of Shem; and Canaan shall be his servant. God shall enlarge Japheth, and he shall dwell in the tents of Shem; and Canaan shall be his servant.'"

Now it seems to us that the most natural inference which a candid reader would make from this passage is, that the curse was denounced against Ham in that branch of his posterity which descended from Canaan. To establish the hypothesis that the curse includes all the posterity of Ham, it appears to us necessary that one of three things be proved to have been the fact. First. It must be proved that the curse was pronounced upon Ham himself; or, secondly, that it was pronounced upon each of his sons individually; or, thirdly, if pronounced upon Canaan, that he was the only offspring of Ham. But we know that no one of these was the fact: whence the inference is obvious. The question we now propose to consider is not whether it is agreeable to our ideas of justice that the offender, Ham, should escape, and the punishment be inflicted upon one of his sons; but whether there exist any just grounds, apart from the reading of our version, for the conclusion that the malediction was uttered against Canaan, and was restricted in its influence to his posterity.

It is said that "Noah awoke from his wine, and knew what his younger son had done unto him." Hebraists tell us that the word rendered *younger* often means, in the original, *little*, and may be so rendered here. Some of the Jewish commentators on this passage say that Canaan, the *little* son, or *grandson* of Noah, first discovered his father's nakedness, and told it to his father Ham, who informed Shem and Japheth. When Noah awoke, knowing what his *younger*, or *little*, son had done unto him, he said: "Cursed be Canaan, a servant of servants shall he be unto his brethren." Other Hebrew scholars, wishing to disprove the explanation of the Rabbins, and thus include Ham, with all his posterity under the curse, tell us that the prophecy is written in Hebrew verse, and, according to the usual licenses in poetical composition, is elliptical: that for the completion of the sentence, *Ham the father of* must be supplied in every instance before the word Canaan; and that this phrase has been supplied in some of the Greek copies of the Old Testament. With this addition, the sentence would stand, "*Cursed be Ham the father of*

Canaan," etc., according to which reading, Ham would really be the subject of the malediction.

But they supply this ellipsis, because, rejecting the hypothesis of the Rabbins, and supposing, as the reading of our version implies, that it was Ham who discovered the nakedness of Noah, they contend that it would have been unjust to have punished Canaan for the iniquity of his father. But would there have been any thing more unjust in this, than in other instances in which God has visited the iniquity of the fathers upon their impenitent children? Does not Jehovah speak of himself as "visiting the iniquity of the fathers upon the children unto the third and fourth generation of them that hate him"? The dying patriarch Jacob, predicting the future condition of his sons, declared to Reuben his first-born, whose crime he particularized, "Unstable as water, thou shalt not excel;" of Simeon and Levi, in consequence of their sins, he said: "I will divide them in Jacob, and scatter them in Israel." (Genesis 49.) But these curses were intended to fall with their full weight, not upon the persons of Reuben, Simeon, and Levi, but upon their posterity. Witness the case of Ahab, whose accumulated and aggravated iniquities incensed the God of Israel against him. The sacred historian informs us that, after the prophet had threatened him with the judgments of God for his transgressions, he showed signs of repentance, whereupon the word of the Lord came to Elijah the Tishbite, saying: "Seest thou how Ahab humbleth himself before me? because he humbleth himself before me, I will not bring the evil in his days: but in his son's days will I bring the evil upon his house." (1 Kings 21 : 28, 29.)

The Jews in the time of our Saviour, seem to have regarded it as a common principle in the Divine operations to visit the iniquity of parents upon their children; hence, their question with reference to the man "blind from his birth." (John 9.) But even if this principle were not manifest in the Divine dealings, would it be any more unjust in the "Judge of all the earth," to punish Canaan for the iniquity of his father, than to proscribe Esau from his rights and privileges before he was born; and, therefore, before, as the Apostle says, he had done either good or evil? There are, however, grounds within the reach of careful investigation, not incompatible with the nature and attributes of God, upon which a satisfactory disposition may be made of these apparent difficulties.

But a rejection of the ellipsis contended for by some, is not essential to the maintaining of our position, for if we admit the ellipsis, it does not appear why the patriarch should have designated Ham, who had several sons, as the *father of Canaan* any more than as the father of any other of his sons, unless it be that the individual is mentioned in connection with Ham, whom the curse is intended to affect, and to whom it was restricted. "Canaan alone in his descendants is cursed, and Ham only in that branch of his posterity."* The curse upon Canaan was properly a curse upon the Canaanites. God, foreseeing the wickedness of this people, commissioned Noah to pronounce a curse upon them, and to devote them to servitude and misery, which their common vices and iniquities would deserve. And this account was plainly written by Moses, for the encouragement of the Israelites, to support and animate them in their expedition against a people who, by their sins, had forfeited the divine protection, and were destined to slavery from the days of Noah.† "It follows,"

---
* Richard Watson.
† Bishop Newton's *Dissertations on the Prophecies.*

says Richard Watson, "that the subjugation of the Canaanitish races fulfills the prophecy."

Let us now notice the events that transpired after the curse, and as recorded in sacred and profane history. The descendants of Canaan peopled that region of country extending along the eastern coast of the Mediterranean. The posterity of Cush, the eldest son of Ham, it is agreed, spread over a great portion of Southern Asia, and first peopled the countries to the south of Egypt, Nubia and Abyssinia, and parts further to the south and west; Mizraim, the second son of Ham, is said to have been the father of the Egyptians. A few hundred years after the utterance of Noah's malediction, we find Jehovah himself uttering a prediction, strangely at variance with the malediction, if the hypothesis that it included Ham and all his posterity be correct.

God said to Abraham, the father of the Jewish nation, who were descendants of Shem: "Know of a surety that thy seed shall be a stranger in a land that is not theirs (in Egypt) and shall serve them; and they (the posterity of Ham) shall afflict them four hundred years." (Genesis 15.) Every one knows the severe bondage which the Israelites endured in Egypt under the Egyptians. The Egyptians were the descendants of Ham; the Jews, the descendants of Shem; the Jews were in servitude to the Egyptians, therefore Shem was the servant of Ham—a palpable reversion of the malediction, if it be true that it included all the posterity of Ham.

Again: Shishak, King of Egypt, a descendant of Ham, subdued Rehoboam, King of Judah, a descendant of Shem, (1 Kings 14 : 25.) It is said that Sesostris, King of Egypt, conquered a great part of Europe and Asia. Here are instances of Ham's prevailing over both

Shem and Japheth. For a long time after the emancipation of the Israelites from Egypt, and even after they had established themselves and gotten a name in Canaan, the Egyptians exercised a considerable influence over their affairs, both political and religious. Even down to the days of King Solomon was this Egyptian influence felt among the Jews, and King Solomon, the wisest of monarchs, was so affected by it, as to violate the commands of God, in order to obey its dictates. (1 Kings 10 : 28, 29; Deut. 17 : 16.) In all this does Shem appear to be ruling Ham? No; it was not the intention of the malediction that either Mizraim or Cush, whose descendants peopled Africa, should be a servant of servants to Shem; but it did intend that the descendants of Canaan, whom it distinctly mentions, should be so related to Shem; and hence, when the cup of iniquity of the Canaanites was full, when, by their own wickedness, they had merited subjugation and extirpation, God brought forth the people whom he designed as the executors of his judgments, from Egyptian bondage, and led them into Canaan; and, as a guarantee to them (for they were ignorant and timid emancipated slaves) that they should overcome the " giants, the sons of Anak, in whose sight they were as grasshoppers,"* he directed Moses to record the malediction: "Cursed be Canaan, a servant of servants shall he be unto his brethren."

The poor Israelites, full of the mental and physical effects of slavery, doubtless approached the confines of the Canaanites, with tremulous steps, in view of conflicts with a formidable people, for which they, mere slaves, or the offspring of slaves, felt entirely unprepared. But as they thus trembled, their minds were

* Numbers 13 : 33.

directed to the prediction: "A servant of servants shall Canaan be unto his brethren." Not a servant of princes; not a servant of warriors; but a servant of servants—of persons precisely in their condition. How peculiarly adapted to them was such a prophecy at that time! How encouraging, as, "on the borders of the Jordan, they

———"Ungered, shivering,
And feared to launch away."

They are animated; they cross the Jordan; city after city of the Canaanites falls before them; tribe after tribe is subdued; until, obtaining possession of the whole land, they reduce the Canaanites either to slavery or extermination. Thus was the prediction of Noah fulfilled. Shem, himself a servant, makes a servant of Canaan, literally verifying the prophecy: "A servant of servants shall he be unto his brethren." In mercy, then, to the Jews of old, was this prophecy recorded, and not to afford grounds to prejudiced and avaricious men for enslaving a people to whom it has no more reference than it has to the descendants of Japheth.

The fact that, in modern times, Africans have been extensively enslaved by other races, is no argument in favor of the hypothesis, which makes them subjects of the malediction; for other peoples, in other parts of the world, have also been and are now enslaved.*

* A Constantinople correspondent of the London *Morning Chronicle* wrote to that paper, in 1854, as follows:

"When I last wrote, I forgot to inclose you the Imperial firmans issued by the Sultan for the suppression of the slave-trade. They read very well, and would tend to persuade strangers that this traffic is really on the point of being put a stop to. The promulgation and execution of a law are two very different things in Turkey. The public slave-market of Constantinople has ceased to exist for some years, but the slave-trade has not diminished. The same number are bought and sold *ad libitum*. The only difference is, that the slave-merchant has his private

There are other causes than the curse pronounced upon Canaan, to which the enslavement of Africans may be and should be referred.

REASONS FOR THE PRESENT CONDITION OF AFRICANS.

The affairs of nations, as of individuals, it must be admitted, are constantly beneath the immediate observation and control of Jehovah, who "doeth according to his will in the army of heaven and among the inhabitants of the earth." His name, as proclaimed by himself, is, "THE LORD GOD, MERCIFUL AND GRACIOUS, LONG-SUFFERING, AND ABUNDANT IN GOODNESS AND TRUTH KEEPING MERCY FOR THOUSANDS, FORGIVING INIQUITY AND TRANSGRESSION AND SIN, AND THAT WILL BY NO MEANS CLEAR THE GUILTY." In the case of no other people has the Almighty more clearly manifested this sublime character, in every feature of it, than in the case of Africans. *He will by no means clear the guilty.* Even in those upon whom he has set his love will he not tolerate transgression. Does Jacob, the Israel of God, commit sin? Notice his subsequent years, and see in their numerous and painful vicissitudes, in his frequent anxieties, fears and distresses — evidences of God's displeasure—castigations for his iniquities. Witness the sin of David, and his subsequent sufferings. Mark also the case of Solomon and others; all of which

---

dwelling. The promulgation of the firman may have some slight influence, but it will be very slight; and it is, therefore, as well to say so, and expose how dust is thrown into the eyes of the European public. . . . As regards the sale and purchase of slaves in Circassia, the desire and ambition of a Circassian girl is to be sold at Constantinople. She has a chance if she is beautiful, of becoming Sultana, or one of the Sultanas, or at least she flatters herself that her good looks will open to her the harem of some opulent Pacha. It must not be disguised that our endeavors to suppress the Circassian slave-trade, though no doubt meritorious, and founded on motives of philanthropy, will be regarded in a very different light by the Circassians, and gain us many an enemy amongst them."

testify to the fact that suffering is consequent upon sin. Indeed, there is no truth more clearly taught in the book of divine revelation, and none more abundantly attested in the history and experience of man, than that punishment is inseparable from crime. God has so arranged things; he has so established the laws both of the physical and moral world, that they can not be violated with impunity. If the violator of the moral law appear not outwardly to suffer, yet he can not effectually shut out from his heart that deep remorse, and those mental distresses which have torment, and which are said to be the forebodings of the "worm that never dies." And this connection of punishment with crime has been noticed by observing and reflecting men of all ages and countries, whether possessing the light of revelation or not. Notice the words of Horace:[*]

> "Raro antecedentem scelestum
> Deseruit pede Pœna claudo."

These lines imply that though the "execution of sentence against an evil work" may be delayed, yet it will certainly overtake the criminal. Punishment is' represented as "slow of foot," yet steadily pursuing the offender. And this law of the moral world is not confined to cases of individuals. Nations sometimes infringe this law, and as nations they suffer. Illustrations of this fact are numerous in the world's history; from the eating of

> —— "The fruit
> Of that forbidden tree, whose mortal taste
> Brought death into the world, and all our woe,"

down to the present time. Witness the destruction of the cities of the plain of Sodom; the extermination of

[*] Another Roman writer says: "Sera tamen tacitis pœna venit pedibus."

the nations of Canaan; the wholesale submersion and extirpation of the Egyptians in the Red Sea; the dispersion and denationalization of the Israelites; the diminished and diminishing numbers of the Indians of North-America; and lastly, the enslavement of Africans—all the effects of sin.

For thousands of years has Africa been without a knowledge of God. While the Egyptians excelled all other nations in their acquaintance with and cultivation of the arts and sciences, they were destitute of the true wisdom. They, as well as other Africans, evidently, at one time, possessed a knowledge of the true God, but they neglected it; and in this consists their crime, that when they knew God, "they glorified him not as God, neither were thankful; they did not like to retain God in their knowledge;" therefore "God gave them over to a reprobate mind, to do those things which are not convenient;" and they fell into all that enormity and blackness of crime which the Apostle so graphically depicts in the first chapter of Romans. And if such was their character in the Apostle's days—two thousand years ago—what must it be now when we consider that human nature left to itself never ameliorates, but grows worse and worse. What an awful picture of depravity and wickedness must present itself to the pure eye of Jehovah!—depravity and wickedness which, brought on by the voluntary acts of the fathers, have been copied and improved upon by the children.

Now the Judge of all the earth would have done no injustice to the Africans had he left them to pursue the course of wickedness entered upon by their fathers, and persevered in by themselves, until, filling up the cup of their iniquity, they had rendered themselves fit vessels of his wrath. But he determined otherwise with respect to this portion of the descendants of Ham; and even while iniquity, like a dense cloud, blackened their moral atmosphere, He, the "Lord God, merciful and gracious, long-suffering and abundant in goodness and truth," gave promises with reference to their wicked land. "Princes shall come out of Egypt; Ethiopia shall soon stretch out her hands unto God." (Psalm 68:31.) "From beyond the rivers of Ethiopia my suppliants, even the daughter of my dispersed, shall bring mine offering." (Zeph. 3:10.)

But Ethiopia is guilty. The guilt of centuries overspreads the whole land, so aggravated and horrible that there can be no communication between its inhabitants and the King of kings. No one of the countless multitudes is seeking for God; no one is asking after his Maker. The Almighty, therefore, in keeping with his character of "by no means clearing the guilty," determines to teach the inhabitants of this dark land "righteousness" by first sending his "judgments" among them. He suffers them to be carried into captivity in fulfillment of a prophecy recorded in Isaiah 18:1, 2: "Woe to the land shadowing with wings, which is beyond the rivers of Ethiopia: that sendeth ambassadors by the sea, even in vessels of bulrushes upon the waters. Go, ye swift messengers, to a nation scattered and peeled, to a people terrible from their beginning hitherto; a nation meted out and trodden down, whose land the rivers have spoiled." For years has He, in his sovereign justice, permitted the cruel traffic in African slaves to be perpetrated with the utmost cruelty on the part of the traders, and unprecedented suffering on the part of the poor African; so that in numerous instances death has seemed preferable to life. And even at this moment poor Africans are groaning beneath intolerable burdens either of physical maltreatment or of mental depression and degradation. Agreeably to the prophecy, we are, indeed, "a nation scattered and peeled, meted out and trodden down," reaping, however, the fruits of our own doings.

But in the chapter in Isaiah just quoted, there is a glorious promise to the scattered people — a promise like shining borders to a black and threatening cloud. Mark the passage, verse seventh, "In that time," the time of their enthrallment, "shall the present be brought unto the Lord of hosts of a people scattered and peeled, and from a people terrible from their beginning hitherto; a nation meted out and trodden under foot, whose land the rivers have spoiled, to the place of the name of the Lord of hosts, the mount of Zion."[*] Are not these prophecies coming to pass? Are not Africans "meted out and trodden down," though they are bringing "presents unto the Lord of hosts," in the land of their captivity? Yes, it is matter of thankfulness that, in the land of their oppression, and in the very depths of their affliction, the Most High, who "is no respecter of persons," has condescended to visit this people, and despite the efforts of their oppressors to debar them from the light of science, God has revealed unto them the "true Light;" while they have been driven away from the streams of earthly learning, they have been welcomed to the very fountain of Knowledge, whence they have had large and "liberal" draughts, without upbraidings. The Holy Spirit has discovered to them their guilt as transgressors of the divine law, and has led them, burdened with the load of sin, to the foot of the same cross to which others resort, where

---

[*] Such an application of this prophecy is objected to by some, but no satisfactory reason is assigned why it should not be so applied.

they have found pardon and peace in believing. They have been clothed with the same robe of the Redeemer's righteousness with which others are clothed, and the same "songs of praises" have been put into their mouths; they have received the same unerring "testimony" that they are the children of God, and they enjoy the same comfortable assurance that if their earthly house of this tabernacle were dissolved, they have a building of God, an house not made with hands, eternal in the heavens. (2 Cor. 5 : 1.) Are not these blessings a glorious compensation for our afflictions? Are they not the "rememberings of mercy in the midst of deserved wrath," for which it becomes us to feel unfeignedly thankful? Yes, there is an inward "peace," a "joy unspeakable," which outward circumstances can not affect. There is a "liberty unsung by poets, which all the powers of earth and hell confederate can not take away." Such "peace," such "joy," such "liberty," many a plantation-slave enjoys.

> —— "The oppressor holds
> His body bound, but knows not what a range
> His spirit takes, unconscious of a chain;
> And that to bind him is a vain attempt,
> Whom God delights in, and in whom he dwells."

Whenever we feel or hear of the oppressions, which men of another race inflict upon us, and the miseries to which they arrogantly subject us, it is natural for feelings of indignation to arise within us against those who are the immediate cause of such sufferings; since we know that they, to gratify pride, prejudice, or malignity, afflict us; not designing good, but evil. But when, upon reflection, we look upon all evils as under the control of God, going no further than he permits them to go; and when we consider what have been our demerits as a people, and that, notwithstanding their enormity, God has been merciful to us, we can not but be grateful. "He has not dealt with us after our sins, neither rewarded us according to our iniquities." He has not dealt so with any nation. Witness his dealings with the Canaanites. He suffered the cup of their iniquity to become full, and then caused them to drink the very dregs thereof, consigning them to the "blackness of darkness forever." Witness the fearful judgments which have befallen the North-American Indians. They have not suffered slavery, but their iniquities have been more severely visited than those of the Africans. They have melted away under the retributive visitations of the Judge of all the earth, leaving no name behind them; perishing in their iniquities without the blessings of the Gospel. But our case has been different. Carried away from home to a distant land, and subjected to a slavery of the most cruel kind, we have survived. We still retain our distinct character as a people, so that it may be said of us, as of the Israelites in Egypt: "The more they afflicted them the more they multiplied and grew." (Exodus 1 : 12.) And may not this fact, so mysterious to many, be solved by the consideration that that all-wise and merciful Providence, which has watched over us in all our afflictions, preserves us for a glorious future destiny? There is now a prospect that, like the Jews, we shall return from our grievous bondage to the land given to our fathers. A small number have already returned—the precursors of a powerful exodus—bearing with them spoils infinitely richer than Egyptian treasure, even the blessings of civilization and of the Christian religion. But we return not as the executors of God's wrath. No; we bear no such fearful message to Africa. We come as the almoners of Heaven's blessings, not to exterminate the inhabitants of the land, but to root up and destroy their iniquities. We come to demolish the kingdom of Satan, and to establish that kingdom which consists in righteousness and peace and "joy in the Holy Ghost:" subjection to whose Sovereign elevates and dignifies human nature; conferring a liberty,

> "———which persecution, fraud,
> Oppressions, prisons, have no power to bind;
> Which whoso tastes can be enslaved no more—
> 'Tis liberty of heart, derived from heaven."

But let it not for one moment be supposed that, because we hold that our oppressions and afflictions are under the immediate permission of God, therefore we justify our oppressors in their cruel treatment of us. By no means. We hold that all men, with respect to each other, are born equally free, having the same "inalienable right to life, liberty, and property;" and that they who, by reason of superior power, assumed authority, or for any other cause deprive their fellow-men of those rights, are robbers, in the strictest sense of that word, and, as such, are guilty and fearfully responsible to the "Judge of all the Earth." We indorse the sentiment of Wordsworth, that

> "Our life is turned
> Out of its course, whenever Man is made
> An offering, or a sacrifice, a tool,
> Or implement, a passive thing employed
> As a brute mean, without acknowledgment
> Of common right or interest in the end."

They who urge the malediction of Noah, to justify themselves in metamorphosing a whole race of men into "offerings," "sacrifices," "tools," "implements," are under a fatal hallucination which, unless they discover it in time for repentance, will sink them "deeper than the grave." They have made themselves the executors of God's judgments, and that not from a desire to glorify him, but to indulge a criminal avarice, which is gratified only by the very life-blood of the African. An American divine,* who hates oppression with a perfect hatred, used the following strong language, on this subject, in a discourse preached in New-York City, October 20, 1856:

"You pretend to be, by charter from Heaven, the ministers of God's vengeance against a whole continent of men — a whole race of mankind — whom, in the execution of that vengeance, you are to hold and sell as your property. You are the trustees of this will of Jehovah, the executors of this inheritance of wrath, and as such you are to be paid for your trouble in proving the instrument, and carrying its details into operation, by assuming the objects of the curse as your property. Where is the sentence in which God ever appointed you, the Anglo-Saxon race, you, the mixture of all races under heaven; you, who can not tell whether the blood of Shem, Ham, or Japheth mingles in your veins; you, the asserters of a right to traffic in human flesh; you, worse than the Jews, by this very claim more degraded, more debased in your moral principles, than the lowest tribes of Jews ever swept for their sins from the Promised Land; where is the sentence in which God ever appointed you, four thousand years after Noah and his children had gone to their graves in peace, to be the executors of Noah's will, with the whole inheritance given to you as your property, for your profit, the reward of your faithfulness in fulfilling God's curse? Where is the designation of the race whom you pounce upon by this mighty forgery, and where the designation of the race commissioned to pounce upon them? You might as well go to Russia and take the subjects of the Czar. You might as well go to England and take your cousins of the sea-girt isle, the descendants of your own great-grandfathers. You have no more claim upon the Africans than you have upon the Aborigines of the Rocky Mountains."

The assumptions of some of the Anglo-Saxons with reference to the African race, are surely unwarrantable. They stultify history, sacred and profane, and set up

* Rev. George B. Cheever, D.D.

theological and philosophical theories in opposition to common-sense, to carry their point. But "the days of arbitrary authority are numbered, and, even in matters of theology, men will think and decide as free and rational beings."

INTELLECTUAL OBTUSENESS,

as a result of Noah's malediction, has been attributed to the African race, as a whole—a traducement which, in consequence of the unfavorable circumstances of the race, has gained considerable currency. But when and where has this been tested and proved? Does it find proof in the case of James McCune Smith, the learned and scientific colored physician of New-York? Is it established in the case of Frederick Douglass, formerly a slave, now a celebrated orator and editor? Where has it been demonstrated? In the cases of Daniel A. Payne, the African theologian and poet, of Cincinnati, and of J. M. Whitfield, poet and editor, of Buffalo? Does the remarkable Miss Frances Watkins, the poetic genius, of Baltimore, afford an illustration? Is there furnished an instance in the celebrated Miss Elizabeth Greenfield, the musical genius of the United States, and the successful rival of Jenny Lind? We might ask similar questions with respect to numerous other Africans, but time would fail us.*

---

* The Rev. John Leighton Wilson, possessed of an extensive experience of African character in its barbarous and uncultured state, records the following testimony: "Some of the best specimens of oratory may be heard in these African assemblies. Their popular speakers show almost as much skill in the use of happy illustrations, striking analogies, pointed argument, historical details, biting irony, as any set of public speakers in the world; and for ease, grace, and naturalness of manner, they are perhaps unsurpassed."—*Western Africa*, p. 142.

The Veys, though not numerous or powerful, have recently invented an alphabet for writing their own language, and are enjoying the blessings of a written sys-

They who circulate the slander of negro intellectual obtuseness, can produce no cases that would fairly and satisfactorily establish their aspersion. They are our oppressors, and, taking us in the midst of our oppression, they fancy they see proofs of their dogma. They find what they regard as moral demonstrations of it, in the cases of "Sambo," and "Juba," and "Topsy," all of corn-field birth, rearing, and notoriety. The inductive method of reasoning is not tolerated in *their* logic with reference to our race. Arguments in our favor which would be regarded as conclusive in regard to any other race, are unceremoniously discarded. Isolated cases the most unfavorable are taken as fair specimens of the character of the whole race. The intellectual and moral character of the African in freedom is infer-

tem, for which they are entirely indebted to their own ingenuity and enterprise. This is, undoubtedly, one of the most remarkable achievements of this or any other age, and is itself enough to silence forever the cavils and sneers of those who think so contemptuously of the intellectual endowments of the African race. The characters used in this system are all new, and were invented by the people themselves within the last twenty years.—*Ibid.* p. 95.

THE NEGRO AND THE NEEDLE.—It is not generally known that for the origin of the needle manufacture we are indebted to the negro. The earliest record of needle-making in England is in the year 1545, in the reign of Henry VIII., and it is supposed that this useful branch of industry was introduced *by a Moor* from Spain. The historian Stowe tells us that needles were sold in Cheapside and other busy streets in London in the reign of Queen Mary, and were at that time made by a *Spanish negro*, who refused to discover the secret of his art. Another authority states that the art of making steel needles was lost at the negro's death, but was afterwards revived by a German in 1566. Probably these facts may account for the crest of the needle-makers' coat-of-arms being the head of a negro.—*American Paper.*

Mr. Aaron Roberts, a colored man in Philadelphia, has invented a valuable aid to the fire department. It is constructed on the principle of a telescope, occupying a very small space when closed, but capable of being extended to a hight of some sixty feet, by means of concealed cogs. Above this is a branch-pipe, made flexible, and worked in any direction by chains reaching the ground. The machine can be run into a narrow alley, and by attaching a hose to a fire-plug, the water will be forced to the top, and thence directed at the pleasure of the operator. Safety is thus afforded to the fireman, and instant application may be made to any part of a burning building.—*The National Magazine,* August, 1856.

red from what it is in slavery, as though the two conditions were exactly similar; or as though the African were not, as other men, influenced by circumstances; so that if the black man, in the midst of cruel oppressions, of which for centuries he has been the subject, gives evidence of the legitimate influences of such oppressions, and does not come forward, though fettered in mind and body, and astonish the world by inventions and discoveries, it follows, according to their reasoning, that, in a condition free and untrammeled, he will be both mentally and physically the same; he is, therefore, set down as belonging to an inferior order of beings, fitted only for servitude—liberty and slavery in their effects upon him, are synonymous and convertible terms. In judging of Anglo-Saxons, one set of principles is applied; in judging of Africans, another.

It can not be truly affirmed that inferences proceeding on such assumptions wait for refutation; but those who avail themselves of them follow *prejudice* more than *judgment*. And so strongly does their prejudice against the African bias their minds, that we often find even the profoundest of them indulging in such one-sided argument. John C. Calhoun, of South Carolina, is lauded to the skies by some, on account of his wonderful powers of induction: and he was, doubtless, on many subjects, a powerful inductive reasoner; yet every one knows the bold and unblushing sophistry which he employed with reference to the African race.*

Let the candid among the enemies of our race, take,

---

* The writer was refused admittance to a literary institution in the United States, on the ground that the faculty had failed to realize their expectations in one or two colored persons whom they had educated. The inductive reasoning here employed was, of course, most conclusive. Some colored persons abuse their education, therefore *all* colored persons should be excluded from institutions of learning. The minor proposition is made to contain the major. Excellent logic!

as far as they know, all the cases of Africans, who have enjoyed any opportunities of intellectual development and improvement, and see if the majority have not profitably availed themselves of those opportunities; or take an African of ordinary mind, and a Caucasian of like capacity, place them both under the same instructions, with equal privileges, and we hazard nothing by saying that the Caucasian will not excel the African, if, indeed, he keep pace with him. This has been tested, and the result has turned out in favor of the African. If, then, under given circumstances, the Caucasian will arrive at a certain point of intellectual improvement, and under the same circumstances, as the facts of a fair induction show, the African will attain to the same point, where is the absolute superiority of the Caucasian? Where is the peculiar mental obtuseness of the African? Where?

"I have often wondered," says our excellent President Benson,* "from whence sprang the silly aspersion of 'the incapacity of the colored race for self-government.' I have frequently taxed my mind for a discovery of the instances upon which the stigma is based. With the exception of our own, Hayti, I believe, is the only professed colored civilized and independent government. It is true, that unfortunate country has been repeatedly convulsed by revolutions and dethronements; but these have neither been restricted nor peculiar to her history; similar causes have produced similar effects among other nations, not of African descent, but purely Caucasian. The South-American States, almost without exception, have been equally prolific of civil wars and revolutions; in fact, we can trace them even into highly civilized Europe, and as not unfrequently occurring among some of the most refined nations of that enlightened continent; nor would proud Albion have been exempted from them, for so long a space as that which has succeeded the seventeenth century, if the Protestant faith, which constitutes the basis of that righteousness which exalts a nation, had not taken so deep root in that country. And if I mistake not, the same cause is to be assigned for the almost unparalleled success with which the confederate States of North-America have been crowned, ... and for lack of which, Hayti, in common with some other governments, to which allusion

* Inaugural Address, January 7th, 1856.

has been made, failed in demonstrating an equal capacity for self-government; and surely the civil wars of Hayti are no more an argument (if as much so) against the capacity of the colored race for self-government, than the multiplied revolutions of the other governments alluded to, are against that of the Caucasian race."

AFRICAN PHYSIOGNOMY.

The physiognomical character of Africans is also urged as an argument in favor of the servile destiny of the race. This being the popular opinion, the greatest unfairness is generally practiced in the representations which Caucasian naturalists and ethnologists make of African features. This may appear a small matter, but we do not deem it altogether unworthy of notice. No matter how men, in their public opinions, may ridicule as absurd arguments thus founded, yet, in their private feelings, they are to a great extent influenced by them. We have observed that, generally in Geographies or books on ethnography, the heads given as proper specimens of the African are pictures of some degraded slaves of poor physical development; while to represent the Caucasian race, the head of some philosopher, or of some very beautiful female is presented as a fair specimen of that whole race. They give " the *highest* type of the European and the *lowest* type of the negro." Now we say this is unjust. That there are irregularities in the African features, is no reason that in representing them the *very worst* should be taken as specimens. This is done, however, to carry out the idea of phrenological inferiority to the other races, at least to the Anglo-Saxon race. Hence, whenever any one of this doomed people gives evidence of superior ability and talents, the disposition is to deny his connection with the genuine negro. No candid and unprejudiced mind can read with patience the unwarrantable description furnished by Mr. Bowen, an American missionary adventurer on this coast, of what he calls "the true or typical negro."* It is a pandering to prejudices entirely unpardonable in one of his profession, whose object should be to eradicate, and not to foster the seed of error. And nothing is more instinctively ridiculous than his labored but resultless endeavor to prove that all the interior native tribes of regular and agreeable features, and of favorable mental characteristics, are the descendants of Europeans. If such are the results of his philosophical and scientific investigations, it would have been more creditable to his reputation, and of less disservice to the cause of truth, to have confined himself to the regions of common-sense.

But the intellectual character of a race can not fairly be argued from the physical appearance of some of its individuals. The external appearance is not always the index of the intellectual man. Notwithstanding the claims and pretensions of phrenology, the old adage should not be neglected: "Judge not of things by their outward appearance."† All scientific writers on the

---

* Bowen's *Central Africa*, chapter xxiii. pp. 280, 281.

† "It was once said that 'No good thing can come out of Nazareth;' and it is now thought that the mere color of the African places him under the general ban of nations, and renders preposterous and absurd the idea that this race could ever have occupied a position of dignity, or contributed to the general advancement of the world. If external aspect (and the assumption admits of triumphant vindication) is considered a mere accident of being, how can it render nugatory all contravening evidence? If so, then reason is a cheat, and Bacon and Newton were sophists! Why the African is black, I know not, nor do I pause to inquire, any more than why you are white. One is as great a mystery to me as the other. It may be the effect of climate and condition; or, what is much more likely, it may be a merciful arrangement of heaven and nature, to prepare them for residence and suffering in the hot intertropical regions assigned them as the bounds of their habitation. I do not profess to be an adept in the science of climatology, nor can I fathom the deep designs of Providence. I leave both to be comprehended and explained by others. But certainly, if the mere extrinsic circumstance, the adventitious adjunct of color is to expel the African from the pale of humanity, of which

subject refer the physical character of Africans to the climate in which they reside, and their peculiar mode and custom of life. In proportion as a people is elevated, or its mode of life cultivated, the features improve, and the whole outward appearance changes; for it is a fact that the degree of the civilization and culture of a people is a fair standard by which to judge of the physical character of that people. A proper education improves the body as well as the mind. Who will undertake to say that the features of the Britons, in the days of Julius Cæsar, were as regular as those of the present inhabitants of England? Give Africans the same amount of culture, from generation to generation, which Europeans have enjoyed, and their features will assume the same proportion and symmetry.

In visiting the native towns interior to Liberia, we have seen, though on a small scale, striking illustrations of this fact. Among the inhabitants of those towns, we could invariably distinguish the free man from the slave. There was about the former a dignity of appearance, an openness of countenance, an independence of air, a firmness of step, which indicated the absence of oppression; while in the latter there was a depression of countenance, a general deformity of appearance, and an awkwardness of gait which seemed to say: "That man is a slave." And it is, for the most part, among the latter class of persons that the slave-trade has found its victims, it being rarely the case that free persons are sold to slave-traders. This will partly account for the general deformity of appearance of the

---

we deem ourselves such fair specimens, the decision reflects but too injuriously upon the magnanimity of earth and the justice of heaven!"—*Posthumous Works of Rev. Henry B. Bascom, D.D., LL.D., one of the Bishops of the M. E. Church, South.*

Africans in the Western hemisphere; going from one form of slavery into another immeasurably more severe, it was impossible that either themselves or their descendants should improve physically. Dr. Prichard, in his researches into the *Physical History of Man*, relates on the authority of Dr. S. S. Smith, of the negroes settled in the Southern districts of the United States of America, that the field-slaves, who live on the plantations, and retain pretty nearly the rude manners of their African progenitors, preserve, in the third generation, much of their original structure, though their features are not so strongly marked as those of imported slaves. But the domestic servants of the same race, who are treated with lenity, and whose condition is little different from that of the lower class of white people, in the third generation have the nose raised, the mouth and lips of moderate size, the eyes lively and sparkling, and often the whole composition of the features extremely agreeable.*

AFRICAN INHERENT LOVE OF SLAVERY.

Another ground of argument with some in favor of the application of Noah's malediction to Africans, and their consequent inferiority to the other races, is the preference for slavery which some emancipated slaves have shown, either refusing to be set at liberty or returning into bondage after having been liberated. But they forget that this is by no means unusual, nor peculiar to the African race. The effect of slavery is to render the mind congenial to itself. Slavery begets in the slave adaptation and attachment to slavery It is a principle of the human mind to love that to which

---

* Watson's *Theological Dictionary*.

long familiarity has accustomed it, particularly if it has been led by any means to believe that the object to which it is accustomed is productive of benefit. How many of the emancipated Israelites would not have returned into Egyptian bondage had they possessed the power and opportunity of so doing? Notwithstanding the manifold and wonderful exhibitions of divine power which attended their exodus from that house of bondage, they were, on the least appearance of trouble, anxious to return. When they wanted bread, listen to their language: "And the children of Israel said, 'Would to God we had died by the hand of the Lord in the land of Egypt, when we sat by the flesh-pots, and when we did eat bread to the full.'" (Exodus 16:3.) When they wanted water, they murmured against Moses their leader, saying: "Wherefore is this that thou hast brought us up out of Egypt to kill us and our children and our cattle with thirst?" (Exodus 17:3.) And, as has been already intimated, even after they had settled in Canaan, and the Lord had extirpated some, and subdued the rest of their enemies, yet they looked to Egypt as their home; and they regarded the Egyptians as superior to themselves even down to the time of Jeremiah. Solomon in all his glory, could not content himself without the daughter of the king of Egypt, for whom he built a splendid palace. (1 Kings 3:1; 7:8.) When, in the days of the prophet Jeremiah, the king of Babylon invaded the land of Judah, a great many of the Jews, contrary to the remonstrances of the prophet, retired into Egypt, as if to their common *home*, saying in answer to the advice of the prophet: "No; but we will go into the land of Egypt, where we shall see no war, nor hear the sound of the trumpet, nor have hunger of bread, and there will we dwell."

Again, when permission was given to the Jews in Babylon to return to Judea from their captivity, and rebuild the temple of the Lord, did they all return? By no means. They had become so wedded to Babylonish habits and modes of life that, though there was so great an inducement to their returning home as the rebuilding of the temple — the "glory of Israel" — yet they would not return. They preferred remaining in the land of their captivity to building up a home for themselves and reëstablishing their nationality.

In view of these facts, then, in the case of a people chosen of God, and blessed above all other peoples in point of religious privileges, shall it be thought wonderful if the same things occur in the case of Africans, a people scattered and peeled, meted out and trodden down? The words of Cowper are universally and incontrovertibly true:

> —— "All constraint,
> Except what wisdom lays on evil men,
> Is evil; hurts the faculties; impedes
> Their progress in the road of science; blinds
> The eyesight of discovery; and begets
> In those who suffer it, a sordid mind,
> Bestial, a meager intellect, unfit
> To be the tenant of man's noble form."

Cases are not wanting of colored persons fleeing from American bondage to Liberia, who, meeting a few difficulties, and unused to the task of self-reliance, wish to return and live their former life of ease and freedom from care. Some do return, and bear back evil reports of this good land. These cases are painful, but they are not surprising; they are illustrations of the invariable effects of slavery. Nor is it to be wondered at that even in Liberia, an African government, free, sovereign, and independent, there should be, as Bishop Scott alleges, "a degree of deference shown to white men that is not shown to colored." This will be the case in every African community for a long time, even after the entire abolition of slavery in the Western world. This reverence of the oppressed for the oppressor, as we have just seen in the case of the Israelites, is not easily shaken off. Such is the influence of the latter upon the former, that their voice on any question has the effect to hush into the profoundest silence the least murmur of dissent on the part of the former.

It is, however, incumbent upon the intelligent among the African race, to discountenance as much as possible this servile feeling, and to use every means to crush it wherever it appears, for its influence on the mind and morals and general progress of the race is fearfully injurious.

INFLUENCE OF THE CURRENT ASPERSIONS UPON OURSELVES, AND OUR DUTY.

If an ignorant man be calumniated, and that calumny be founded upon facts of Theology, Science, or Philosophy, branches of learning with which he is, of course, utterly unacquainted, it will not be surprising if that man, even with the facts of his own consciousness before him, contradictory of such calumny, should believe it, and shape his course of conduct in accordance with its *dicta*. So has it been, generally speaking, with the African race. We have been under those whose interest it was to give credit, importance, and circulation to the current aspersions against our race; and who, having all the influence over us which education, wealth, and power can confer, have succeeded too well in working in the minds of many the belief that we are a people accursed, and that, in consequence, we are in every respect inferior to them, and never can, by any combination of fortuitous circumstances, rise to perfect equality with them. Hence we see many ignorant and unfortunate persons of color under the poisoning influence of this inculcated belief, who make no effort towards improvement, believing that their state has been fixed by an irreversible decree — a state of unconditional inferiority to the Caucasian. There is among such persons a constant distrust of each other; a disposition to repose with greater confidence in persons of another race; a want of faith in any thing remarkable done or projected by their own people. Galileans themselves, they doubt their own capacity for the production of "any good thing," and for no other reason than that it is currently reported that "no good thing can come out of Galilea."

It is earnestly to be hoped that in the republic of Liberia no such feeling will exist. Nothing can be more detrimental to our progress. It will act like an incubus upon our energies. Let us, when our brethren come among us from the land of bondage, poisoned with the opinion of the inferiority of the African race, endeavor as soon as possible to eradicate the notion. And let us teach our children from their infancy — for they need to be taught — that no curse except that which every day follows the impenitent, hangs upon us; that it is the force of circumstances, induced, as we have endeavored to show, by our iniquities, that keeps us down; and that we have as much right as any other people to strive to rise to the very zenith of national glory. "Already has the auspicious day of the national glory of our race begun to dawn; it has been divinely and mysteriously brought about; it is the work of Almighty God, and marvelous in our eyes; and this has emboldened me to say that if this government unswervingly pursue a course of sound policy founded on religion and virtue, we shall not, we can not, we will not fail of success; for we shall then clearly comprehend the force of the expression, 'How shall those be cursed whom God hath not cursed?' or, in other words, the impossibility will appear of keeping any nation or people buried in everlasting degradation and contempt for whose exaltation the arm of Omnipotence is manifestly stretched forth."[*]

The position of the people of Liberia invests them with peculiar ability for doing good in behalf of the down-trodden race to which they belong. If they properly use that ability, they may exert no inconsiderable influence in bringing about the universal disenthrallment and elevation of Africans. They should not, in order to benefit their enslaved brethren, "render evil for evil" to their oppressors. Such a course is productive of no good; it is a plan of procedure that finds no sympathy in these enlightened days; it is a progeny of the dark ages. These are times when, by argumentation and demonstration, the moral sensibilities of men must be appealed to. Physical inconveniences, employed for the purpose of correcting moral evils, have no true reformatory effect. Men must be *led*, not *driven*. No desirable effect can be produced by reiterating doleful complaints and harsh vituperations against men on account of their prejudices. But a great deal is accomplished by furnishing practical demonstrations that such prejudices are destitute of foundation. And

---
[*] Message of President Benson, December 4th, 1854.

this is the work of the people of Liberia in particular, and of colored men in general. We must *prove* to our oppressors that we are men, possessed of like susceptibilities with themselves; by seeking after those attributes which give dignity to a state; by cultivating those virtues which shed lustre upon individuals and communities; by pursuing whatever is magnificent in enterprise, whatever is lovely and of good report in civilization, whatever is exalted in morals, and whatever is exemplary in piety. Then shall we prove that we *do* possess "rights which white people are bound to respect," the decision of an enlightened Chief-Justice to the contrary notwithstanding. But so long as we contentedly remain at the foot of the ladder at whose top our oppressors stand, it is unreasonable, it is absurd to call upon them to recognize us as equals in every respect; and it is worse than absurdity to abuse and vilify them for their opinions and prejudices with respect to us. We must make our way to the position which they occupy. And having overstepped the interval which has so long separated us from them, and standing with them on the same summit, we shall be welcomed as equals. Then will Shem, Ham, and Japheth dwell together as brethren, in "liberty, equality, and fraternity." There will be no more slavery, for Canaan, the "servant of servants," has been exterminated.

THE CALL OF PROVIDENCE
TO THE
Descendants of Africa in America.
A DISCOURSE

DELIVERED TO COLORED CONGREGATIONS IN THE CITIES OF NEW-YORK, PHILADELPHIA, BALTIMORE, HARRISBURGH, ETC., DURING THE SUMMER OF 1862.

THE CALL OF PROVIDENCE

TO THE

Descendants of Africa in America.

"BEHOLD, the Lord thy God hath set the land before thee: go up and possess it, as the Lord God of thy fathers hath said unto thee; fear not, neither be discouraged."—DEUTERONOMY 1 : 21.

AMONG the descendants of Africa in this country the persuasion seems to prevail, though not now to the same extent as formerly, that they owe no special duty to the land of their forefathers; that their ancestors having been brought to this country against their will, and themselves having been born in the land, they are in duty bound to remain here and give their attention exclusively to the acquiring for themselves, and perpetuating to their posterity, social and political rights, notwithstanding the urgency of the call which their fatherland, by its forlorn and degraded moral condition, makes upon them for their assistance.

All other people feel a pride in their ancestral land, and do every thing in their power to create for it, if it has not already, an honorable name. But many of the descendants of Africa, on the contrary, speak disparagingly of their country; are ashamed to acknowledge any connection with that land, and would turn indignantly upon any who would bid them go up and take possession of the land of their fathers.

It is a sad feature in the residence of Africans in this country, that it has begotten in them a forgetfulness of Africa—a want of sympathy with her in her moral and intellectual desolation, and a clinging to the land which for centuries has been the scene of their thralldom. A shrewd European observer[*] of American society, says of the negro in this country, that he "makes a thousand fruitless efforts to insinuate himself among men who repulse him; he conforms to the taste of his oppressors, adopts their opinions, and hopes by imitating them to form a part of their community. Having been told from infancy that his race is naturally inferior to that of the whites, he assents to the proposition, and is ashamed of his own nature. In each of his features he discovers a trace of slavery, and, if it were in his power, he would willingly rid himself of every thing that makes him what he is."

It can not be denied that some very important advantages have accrued to the black man from his deportation to this land, but it has been at the expense of his manhood. Our nature in this country is not the same as it appears among the lordly natives of the interior of Africa, who have never felt the trammels of a foreign yoke. We have been dragged into depths of degradation. We have been taught a cringing servility. We have been drilled into contentment with the most undignified circumstances. Our finer sensibilities have been blunted. There has been an almost utter extinction of all that delicacy of feeling and sentiment which adorns character. The temperament of our souls has become harder or coarser, so that we can walk forth here, in this land of indignities, in ease and in complacency, while our complexion furnishes ground for every

---

[*] De Tocqueville, *Democracy in America*.

species of social insult which an intolerant prejudice may choose to inflict.

But a change is coming over us. The tendency of events is directing the attention of the colored people to some other scene, and Africa is beginning to receive the attention, which has so long been turned away from her; and as she throws open her portals and shows the inexhaustible means of comfort and independence within, the black man begins to feel dissatisfied with the annoyances by which he is here surrounded, and looks with longing eyes to his fatherland. I venture to predict that, within a very brief period, that down-trodden land instead of being regarded with prejudice and distaste, will largely attract the attention and engage the warmest interest of every man of color. A few have always sympathized with Africa, but it has been an indolent and unmeaning sympathy—a sympathy which put forth no effort, made no sacrifices, endured no self-denial, braved no obloquy for the sake of advancing African interests. But the scale is turning, and Africa is becoming the all-absorbing topic.

It is my desire, on the present occasion, to endeavor to set before you the work which, it is becoming more and more apparent, devolves upon the black men of the United States; and to guide my thoughts, I have chosen the words of the text: "Behold, the Lord thy God hath set the land before thee: go up and possess it, as the Lord God of thy fathers hath said unto thee; fear not, neither be discouraged."

You will at once perceive that I do not believe that the work to be done by black men is in this country. I believe that their field of operation is in some other and distant scene. Their work is far nobler and loftier than that which they are now doing in this country.

It is theirs to betake themselves to injured Africa, and bless those outraged shores, and quiet those distracted families with the blessings of Christianity and civilization. It is theirs to bear with them to that land the arts of industry and peace, and counteract the influence of those horrid abominations which an inhuman avarice has introduced—to roll back the appalling cloud of ignorance and superstition which overspreads the land, and to rear on those shores an asylum of liberty for the down-trodden sons of Africa wherever found. This is the work to which Providence is obviously calling the black men of this country.

I am aware that some, against all experience, are hoping for the day when they will enjoy equal social and political rights in this land. We do not blame them for so believing and trusting. But we would remind them that there is a faith against reason, against experience, which consists in believing or pretending to believe very important propositions upon very slender proofs, and in maintaining opinions without any proper grounds. It ought to be clear to every thinking and impartial mind, that there can never occur in this country an equality, social or political, between whites and blacks. The whites have for a long time had the advantage. All the affairs of the country are in their hands. They make and administer the laws; they teach the schools; here, in the North, they ply all the trades, they own all the stores, they have possession of all the banks, they own all the ships and navigate them; they are the printers, proprietors, and editors of the leading newspapers, and they shape public opinion. Having always had the lead, they have acquired an ascendency they will ever maintain. The blacks have very few or no agencies in operation to counteract the ascendant influence of the Europeans. And instead of employing what little they have by a unity of effort to alleviate their condition, they turn all their power against themselves by their endless jealousies, and rivalries, and competition; every one who is able to "pass" being emulous of a place among Europeans or Indians. This is the effect of their circumstances. It is the influence of the dominant class upon them. It argues no essential inferiority in them—no more than the disadvantages of the Israelites in Egypt argued their essential inferiority to the Egyptians. They are the weaker class overshadowed and depressed by the stronger. They are the feeble oak dwarfed by the overspreadings of a large tree, having not the advantage of rain, and sunshine, and fertilizing dews.

Before the weaker people God has set the land of their forefathers, and bids them go up and possess it without fear or discouragement. Before the tender plant he sets an open field, where, in the unobstructed air and sunshine, it may grow and flourish in all its native luxuriance.

There are two ways in which God speaks to men: one is by his word and the other by his providence. He has not sent any Moses, with signs and wonders, to cause an exodus of the descendants of Africa to their fatherland, yet he has loudly spoken to them as to their duty in the matter. He has spoken by his providence. First; By suffering them to be brought here and placed in circumstances where they could receive a training fitting them for the work of civilizing and evangelizing the land whence they were torn, and by preserving them under the severest trials and afflictions. Secondly; By allowing them, notwithstanding all the services they have rendered to this country, to be treated as strangers and aliens, so as to cause them to have anguish of spirit, as was the case with the Jews in Egypt, and to make them long for some refuge from their social and civil deprivations. Thirdly; By bearing a portion of them across the tempestuous seas back to Africa, by preserving them through the process of acclimation, and by establishing them in the land, despite the attempts of misguided men to drive them away. Fourthly; By keeping their fatherland in reserve for them in their absence.

The manner in which Africa has been kept from invasion is truly astounding. Known for ages, it is yet unknown. For centuries its inhabitants have been the victims of the cupidity of foreigners. The country has been rifled of its population. It has been left in some portions almost wholly unoccupied, but it has remained unmolested by foreigners. It has been very near the crowded countries of the world, yet none has relieved itself to any great extent of its overflowing population by seizing upon its domains. Europe, from the North, looks wishfully and with longing eyes across the narrow straits of Gibraltar. Asia, with its teeming millions, is connected with us by an isthmus wide enough to admit of her throwing thousands into that country. But, notwithstanding the known wealth of the resources of the land, of which the report has gone into all the earth, there is still a terrible vail between us and our neighbors, the all-conquering Europeans, which they are only now essaying to lift; while the teeming millions of Asia have not even attempted to leave their boundaries to penetrate our borders. Neither alluring visions of glorious conquests, nor brilliant hopes of rapid enrichment, could induce them to invade the country. It has been preserved alike from the boastful civilization of Europe, and the effete and barbarous institutions of Asia. We call it, then, a Providential interposition, that while the owners of the soil have been abroad, passing through the fearful ordeal of a most grinding oppression, the land, though entirely unprotected, has lain uninvaded. We regard it as a providential call to Africans every where, to " go up and possess the land;" so that in a sense that is not merely constructive and figurative, but truly literal, God says to the black men of this country, with reference to Africa: " Behold, I set the land before you, go up and possess it."

Of course it can not be expected that this subject of the duty of colored men to go up and take possession of their fatherland, will be at once clear to every mind. Men look at objects from different points of view, and form their opinions according to the points from which they look, and are guided in their actions according to the opinions they form. As I have already said, the majority of exiled Africans do not seem to appreciate the great privilege of going and taking possession of the land. They seem to have lost all interest in that land, and to prefer living in subordinate and inferior positions in a strange land among oppressors, to encountering the risks involved in emigrating to a distant country. As I walk the streets of these cities, visit the hotels, go on board the steamboats, I am grieved to notice how much intelligence, how much strength and energy is frittered away in those trifling employments, which, if thrown into Africa, might elevate the millions of that land from their degradation, tribes at a time, and create an African power which would command the respect of the world, and place in the possession of Africans, its rightful owners, the wealth which is now diverted to other quarters. Most of the wealth that could be drawn from that land, during the last six centuries, has passed into the hands of Europeans, while many of Africa's own sons, sufficiently intelligent to control those immense resources, are sitting down in poverty and dependence in the land of strangers—exiles when they have so rich a domain from which they have never been expatriated, but which is willing, nay, anxious to welcome them home again.

We need some African power, some great center of the race where our physical, pecuniary, and intellectual strength may be collected. We need some spot whence such an influence may go forth in behalf of the race as shall be felt by the nations. We are now so scattered and divided that we can do nothing. The imposition begun last year by a foreign power upon Hayti, and which is still persisted in, fills every black man who has heard of it with indignation, but we are not strong enough to speak out effectually for that land. When the same power attempted an outrage upon the Liberians, there was no African power strong enough to interpose. So long as we remain thus divided, we may expect impositions. So long as we live simply by the sufferance of the nations, we must expect to be subject to their caprices.

Among the free portion of the descendants of Africa, numbering about four or five millions, there is enough talent, wealth, and enterprise, to form a respectable nationality on the continent of Africa. For nigh three hundred years their skill and industry have been expended in building up the southern countries of the New World, the poor, frail constitution of the Caucasian not allowing him to endure the fatigue and toil involved in such labors. Africans and their descendants have been the laborers, and the mechanics, and the artisans in the greater portion of this hemisphere. By the results of their labor the European countries have been sustained and enriched. All the cotton, coffee, indigo, sugar, tobacco, etc., which have formed the most important articles of European commerce, have been raised and prepared for market by the labor of the black man. Dr. Palmer of New-Orleans, bears the same testimony.* And all this labor they have done, for the most part not only without compensation, but with abuse, and contempt, and insult, as their reward.

Now, while Europeans are looking to our fatherland with such eagerness of desire, and are hastening to explore and take away its riches, ought not Africans in the Western hemisphere to turn their regards thither also? We need to collect the scattered forces of the race, and there is no rallying-ground more favorable than Africa. There

"No pent-up Utica contracts our powers,
The whole boundless continent is ours."

Ours as a gift from the Almighty when he drove asunder the nations and assigned them their boundaries; and ours by peculiar physical adaptation.

An African nationality is our great need, and God tells us by his providence that he has set the land before us, and bids us go up and possess it. We shall never receive the respect of other races until we establish a powerful nationality. We should not content ourselves with living among other races, simply by their permission or their endurance, as Africans live in this country. We must build up negro states; we must establish and maintain the various institutions; we must make and administer laws, erect and preserve churches, and support the worship of God; we must

* In the famous sermon of this distinguished divine on *Slavery a Divine Trust*, he says: "The enriching commerce which has built the splendid cities and marble palaces of England as well as of America, has been largely established upon the products of Southern soil; and the blooms upon Southern fields, gathered by black hands, have fed the spindles and looms of Manchester and Birmingham not less than of Lawrence and Lowell."

have governments; we must have legislation of our own; we must build ships and navigate them; we must ply the trades, instruct the schools, control the press, and thus aid in shaping the opinions and guiding the destinies of mankind. Nationality is an ordinance of Nature. The heart of every true negro yearns after a distinct and separate nationality.

Impoverished, feeble, and alone, Liberia is striving to establish and build up such a nationality in the home of the race. Can any descendant of Africa turn contemptuously upon a scene where such efforts are making? Would not every right-thinking negro rather lift up his voice and direct the attention of his brethren to that land? Liberia, with outstretched arms, earnestly invites all to come. We call them forth out of all nations; we bid them take up their all and leave the countries of their exile, as of old the Israelites went forth from Egypt, taking with them their trades and their treasures, their intelligence, their mastery of arts, their knowledge of the sciences, their practical wisdom, and every thing that will render them useful in building up a nationality. We summon them from these States, from the Canadas, from the East and West-Indies, from South-America, from every where, to come and take part with us in our great work.

But those whom we call are under the influence of various opinions, having different and conflicting views of their relations and duty to Africa, according to the different stand-points they occupy. So it was with another people who, like ourselves, were suffering from the effects of protracted thralldom, when on the borders of the land to which God was leading them. When Moses sent out spies to search the land of Canaan, every man, on his return, seemed to be influenced in his report by his peculiar temperament, previous habits of thought, by the degree of his physical courage, or by something peculiar in his point of observation. All agreed, indeed, that it was an exceedingly rich land, "flowing with milk and honey," for they carried with them on their return, a proof of its amazing fertility. But a part, and a larger part, too, saw only giants and walled towns, and barbarians and cannibals. "Surely," said they, "it floweth with milk and honey. Nevertheless the people be strong that dwell in the land, and the cities are walled, and very great; and moreover we saw the children of Anak there. The land through which we have gone to search it, is a land that eateth up the inhabitants thereof; and all the people that we saw in it are men of a great stature. And there we saw the giants, the sons of Anak, which come of the giants: and we were in our own sight as grasshoppers, and so we were in their sight." It was only a small minority of that company that saw things in a more favorable light. "Caleb stilled the people before Moses, and said, Let us go up at once and possess it; for we be well able to overcome it." (Numbers 13.)

In like manner there is division among the colored people of this country with regard to Africa, that land which the providence of God is bidding them go up and possess. Spies sent from different sections of this country by the colored people — and many a spy not commissioned — have gone to that land, and have returned and reported. Like the Hebrew spies, they have put forth diverse views. Most believe Africa to be a fertile and rich country, and an African nationality a desirable thing. But some affirm that the land is not fit to dwell in, for "it is a land that eateth up the inhabitants thereof," notwithstanding the millions of strong and vigorous aborigines who throng all parts of the country, and the thousands of colonists who are settled along the coast; some see in the inhabitants incorrigible barbarism, degradation, and superstition, and insuperable hostility to civilization; others suggest that the dangers and risks to be encountered, and the self-denial to be endured, are too great for the slender advantages which, as it appears to them, will accrue from immigration. A few only report that the land is open to us on every hand—that "every prospect pleases," and that the natives are so tractable that it would be a comparatively easy matter for civilized and Christianized black men to secure all the land to Christian law, liberty, and civilization.

I come to-day to defend the report of the minority. The thousands of our own race, emigrants from this country, settled for more than forty years in that land, agree with the minority report. Dr. Barth, and other travelers to the east and south-east of Liberia, indorse the sentiment of the minority, and testify to the beauty, and healthfulness, and productiveness of the country, and to the mildness and hospitality of its inhabitants. In Liberia we hear from natives, who are constantly coming to our settlements from the far interior, of land exuberantly fertile, of large, numerous, and wealthy tribes, athletic and industrious; not the descendants of Europeans—according to Bowen's insane theory—but *black* men, pure negroes, who live in large towns, cultivate the soil, and carry on extensive traffic, maintaining amicable relations with each other and with men from a distance.

The ideas that formerly prevailed of the interior of Africa, which suited the purposes of poetry and sensation writing, have been proved entirely erroneous. Poets may no longer sing with impunity of Africa:

> "A region of drought, where no river glides,
> Nor rippling brook with osiered sides;
> Where sedgy pool, nor bubbling fount,
> Nor tree, nor cloud, nor misty mount,
> Appears to refresh the aching eye,
> But barren earth and the burning sky,
> And the blank horizon round and round."

No; missionary and scientific enterprises have disproved such fallacies. The land possesses every possible inducement. That extensive and beauteous domain which God has given us appeals to us and to black men every where, by its many blissful and benignant aspects; by its flowery landscapes, its beautiful rivers, its serene and peaceful skies; by all that attractive and perennial verdure which overspreads the hills and valleys; by its every prospect lighted up by delightful sunshine; by all its natural charms, it calls upon us to rescue it from the grasp of remorseless superstition, and introduce the blessings of the Gospel.

But there are some among the intelligent colored people of this country who, while they profess to have great love for Africa, and tell us that their souls are kindled when they hear of their fatherland, yet object to going themselves, because, as they affirm, the black man has a work to accomplish in this land — he has a destiny to fulfill. He, the representative of Africa, like the representatives from various parts of Europe, must act his part in building up this great composite nation. It is not difficult to see what the work of the black man is in this land. The most inexperienced observer may at once read his destiny. Look at the various departments of society here in the *free* North; look at the different branches of industry, and see how the black man is aiding to build up this nation. Look at the hotels, the saloons, the steamboats, the barbershops, and see how successfully he is carrying out his destiny! And there is an extreme likelihood that such are forever to be the exploits which he is destined to achieve in this country until he merges his African peculiarities in the Caucasian.

Others object to the *climate* of Africa, first, that it is unhealthy, and secondly, that it is not favorable to intellectual progress. To the first, we reply that it is not more insalubrious than other new countries. Persons going to Africa, who have not been broken down as to their constitutions in this country, stand as fair a chance of successful acclimation as in any other country of large, unbroken forests and extensively uncleared lands. In all new countries there are sufferings and privations. All those countries which have grown up during the last two centuries, in this hemisphere, have had as a foundation the groans, and tears, and blood of the pioneers. But what are the sufferings of pioneers, compared with the greatness of the results they accomplish for succeeding generations? Scarcely any great step in human progress is made without multitudes of victims. Every revolution that has been effected, every nationality that has been established, every country that has been rescued from the abominations of savagism, every colony that has been planted, has involved perplexities and sufferings to the generation who undertook it. In the evangelization of Africa, in the erection of African nationalities, we can expect no exceptions. The man, then, who is not able to suffer and to die for his fellows when necessity requires it, is not fit to be a pioneer in this great work.

We believe, as we have said, that the establishment of an African nationality in Africa is the great need of the African race; and the men who have gone, or may hereafter go to assist in laying the foundations of empire, so far from being dupes, or cowards, or traitors, as some have ignorantly called them, are the truest heroes of the race. They are the soldiers rushing first into the breach—physicians who at the risk of their own lives are first to explore an infectious disease. How much more nobly do they act than those who have held for years that it is nobler to sit here and patiently suffer with our brethren! Such sentimental inactivity finds no respect in these days of rapid movement. The world sees no merit in mere innocence. The man who contents himself to sit down and exemplify the virtue of patience and endurance will find no sympathy from the busy, restless crowd that rush by him. Even the "sick man" must get out of the way when he hears the tramp of the approaching host, or be crushed by the heedless and massive car of progress. Blind Bartimeuses are silenced by the crowd. The world requires active service; it respects only productive workers. The days of hermits and monks have passed away. Action—work, work—is the order of the day. Heroes in the strife and struggle of humanity are the demand of the age.

"They who would be free, *themselves* must strike the blow."

With regard to the objection founded upon the unfavorableness of the climate to intellectual progress, I have only to say, that proper moral agencies, when set in operation, can not be overborne by physical causes. "We continually behold lower laws held in restraint by higher; mechanic by dynamic; chemical by vital; physical by moral."* It has not yet been proved that with the proper influences, the tropics will not produce

* Dean Trench, quoted by Baden Powell in *Essays and Reviews*, 1861.

men of "cerebral activity." Those races which have degenerated by a removal from the North to the tropics did not possess the proper moral power. They had in themselves the seed of degeneracy, and would have degenerated any where. It was not Anglo-Saxon blood, nor a temperate climate, that kept the first emigrants to this land from falling into the same indolence and inefficiency which have overtaken the European settlers in South America, but the Anglo-Saxon Bible — the principles contained in that book, are the great conservative and elevating power. Man is the same, and the human mind is the same, whether existing beneath African suns or Arctic frosts. I can conceive of no difference. It is the moral influences brought to bear upon the man that make the difference in his progress.

"High degrees of moral sentiment," says a distinguished American writer,* "control the unfavorable influences of climate; and some of our grandest examples of men and of races come from the equatorial regions." Man is elevated by taking hold of that which is higher than himself. Unless this is done, climate, color, race, will avail nothing.

"——unless above himself he can
Erect himself, how poor a thing is man!"

For my own part, I believe that the brilliant world of the tropics, with its marvels of nature, must of necessity give to mankind a new career of letters, and new forms in the various arts, whenever the millions of men at present uncultivated shall enjoy the advantages of civilization.

Africa will furnish a development of civilization which the world has never yet witnessed. Its great

* R. W. Emerson, in the *Atlantic Monthly*, April, 1862.

peculiarity will be its moral element. The Gospel is to achieve some of its most beautiful triumphs in that land. "God shall enlarge Japheth, and he shall dwell in the tents of Shem," was the blessing upon the European and Asiatic races. Wonderfully have these predictions been fulfilled. The all-conquering descendants of Japheth have gone to every clime, and have planted themselves on almost every shore. By means fair and unfair, they have spread themselves, have grown wealthy and powerful. They have been truly "enlarged." God has "dwelt in the tents of Shem," for so some understand the passage. The Messiah—God manifest in the flesh—was of the tribe of Judah. He was born and dwelt in the tents of Shem. The promise to Ethiopia, or Ham, is like that to Shem, of a spiritual kind. It refers not to physical strength, not to large and extensive domains, not to foreign conquests, not to wide-spread domination, but to the possession of spiritual qualities, to the elevation of the soul heavenward, to spiritual aspirations and divine communications. "Ethiopia shall stretch forth her hands unto God." Blessed, glorious promise! Our trust is not to be in chariots or horses, not in our own skill or power, but our help is to be in the name of the Lord. And surely, in reviewing our history as a people, whether we consider our preservation in the lands of our exile, or the preservation of our fatherland from invasion, we are compelled to exclaim: "Hitherto hath the Lord helped us!" Let us, then, fear not the influences of climate. Let us go forth stretching out our hands to God, and if it be as hot as Nebuchadnezzar's furnace, there will be one in the midst like unto the Son of God, counteracting its deleterious influences.

Behold, then, the Lord our God has set the land before us, with its burning climate, with its privations, with its moral, intellectual, and political needs, and by his providence he bids us go up and possess it without fear or discouragement. Shall we go up at his bidding ? If the black men of this country, through unbelief or indolence, or for any other cause, fail to lay hold of the blessings which God is proffering to them, and neglect to accomplish the work which devolves upon them, the work will be done, but others will be brought in to do it, and to take possession of the country.

For while the colored people here are tossed about by various and conflicting opinions as to their duty to that land, men are going thither from other quarters of the globe. They are entering the land from various quarters with various motives and designs, and may eventually so preöccupy the land as to cut us off from the fair inheritance which lies before us, unless we go forth without further delay and establish ourselves.

The enterprise and energy manifested by white men who, with uncongenial constitutions, go from a distance to endeavor to open up that land to the world, are far from creditable to the civilized and enlightened colored men of the United States, when contrasted with their indifference in the matter. A noble army of self-expatriated evangelists have gone to that land from Europe and America; and, while anxious to extend the blessings of true religion, they have in no slight degree promoted the cause of science and commerce. Many have fallen, either from the effects of the climate or by the hands of violence;[*] still the interest in the land is by

---

[*] The names of John Ledyard, Frederick Horneman, Dr. Walter Oudney, Captain Clapperton, Major Denman, John Richardson, and Dr. Overweg occur in the list of those who have fallen victims either to the climate or the hardships of their pilgrimage. But a more melancholy enumeration may be made. Major Houghton

no means diminished. The enamored worshiper of science, and the Christian philanthropist, are still laboring to solve the problem of African geography, and to elevate its benighted tribes. They are not only disclosing to the world the mysteries of regions hitherto unexplored, but tribes whose very existence had not before been known to the civilized world have been brought, through their instrumentality, into contact with civilization and Christianity. They have discovered in the distant portions of that land countries as productive as any in Europe and America. They have informed the world of bold and lofty mountains, extensive lakes, noble rivers, falls rivaling Niagara, so that, as a result of their arduous, difficult, and philanthropic labors of exploration, the cause of Christianity, ethnology, geography, and commerce has been, in a very important degree, subserved.

Dr. Livingstone, the indefatigable African explorer, who, it is estimated, has passed over not less than eleven thousand miles of African ground, speaking of the motives which led him to those shores, and still keep him there in spite of privations and severe afflictions, says:

"I expect to find for myself no large fortune in that country; nor do I expect to explore any large portions of a new country; but I do hope to find a pathway, by means of the river Zambesi, which may lead to highlands, where Europeans may form a settlement, and where, by opening up communication and establishing commercial intercourse with the natives of Africa, they may slowly, but not the less surely, impart to the people of that country the knowledge and inestimable blessings of Christianity."

perished, or was murdered, in the basin of the Gambia. The truly admirable Mungo Park was killed in an attack of the natives, at a difficult passage of the Niger. The same fate befell Richard Lander in the lower course of the river. Major Laing was foully slain in his tent at a halting-place in the Sahara. John Davidson was assassinated soon after passing the fringe of the desert. Dr. Cowan and Captain Donovan disappeared in the wilds of South-Africa. Dr. Vogel was assassinated in the country about Lake Chad.—*Leisure Hour.*

The recently formed Oxford, Cambridge, and Dublin Missionary Society state their object to be to spread Christianity among the untaught people of Central Africa, "so to operate among them as by mere teaching and influence to help *to build up native Christian states.*" The idea of building up "native Christian states" is a very important one, and is exactly such an idea as would be carried out if there were a large influx of civilized blacks from abroad.

I am sorry to find that among some in this country, the opinion prevails that in Liberia a distinction is maintained between the colonists and the aborigines, so that the latter are shut out from the social and political privileges of the former. No candid person who has read the laws of Liberia, or who has visited that country, can affirm or believe such a thing. The idea no doubt arises from the fact that the aborigines of a country generally suffer from the settling of colonists among them. But the work of Liberia is somewhat different from that of other colonies which have been planted on foreign shores. The work achieved by other emigrants has usually been—the enhancement of their own immediate interests; the increase of their physical comforts and conveniences; the enlargement of their borders by the most speedy and available methods, without regard to the effect such a course might have upon the aborigines. Their interests sometimes coming into direct contact with those of the owners of the soil, they have not unfrequently, by their superior skill and power, reduced the poor native to servitude or complete annihilation. The Israelites could live in peace in the land of Canaan only by exterminating the indigenous inhabitants. The colony that went out from Phenicia, and that laid the foundations of empire on the northern shores of Africa, at first paid a yearly tax to the natives; with the increasing wealth and power of Carthage, however, the respective conditions of the Carthaginians and the natives were changed, and the Phenician adventurers assumed and maintained a dominion over the Libyans. The colonies from Europe which landed at Plymouth Rock, at Boston, and at Jamestown—which took possession of the West-India islands and of Mexico, treated the aborigines in the same manner. The natives of India, Australia, and New-Zealand are experiencing a similar treatment under the overpowering and domineering rule of the Anglo-Saxons. Eagerness for gain and the passion for territorial aggrandisement have appeared to the colonists necessary to their growth and progress.

The work of Liberia, as I have said, is different and far nobler. We, on the borders of our fatherland, can not, as the framers of our Constitution wisely intimated, allow ourselves to be influenced by "avaricious speculations," or by desires for "territorial aggrandisement." Our work there is moral and intellectual as well as physical. We have to work upon the *people*, as well as upon the *land*—upon *mind* as well as upon *matter*. Our prosperity depends as much upon the wholesome and elevating influence we exert upon the native population, as upon the progress we make in agriculture, commerce, and manufacture. Indeed the conviction prevails in Liberia among the thinking people that we can make no important progress in these things without the coöperation of the aborigines. We believe that no policy can be more suicidal in Liberia than that which would keep aloof from the natives around us. We believe that our life and strength will be to elevate and incorporate them among us as speedily as possible.

And, then, the aborigines are not a race alien from

the colonists. We are a part of them. When alien and hostile races have come together, as we have just seen, one has had to succumb to the other; but when different peoples of the same family have been brought together, there has invariably been a fusion, and the result has been an improved and powerful class. When three branches of the great Teutonic family met on the soil of England, they united. It is true that at first there was a distinction of caste among them in consequence of the superiority in every respect of the great Norman people; but, as the others came up to their level, the distinctions were quietly effaced, and Norman, Saxon, and Dane easily amalgamated. Thus, "a people inferior to none existing in the world was formed by the mixture of three branches of the great Teutonic family with each other and the aboriginal Britons."*

In America we see how readily persons from all parts of Europe assimilate; but what great difficulty the Negro, the Chinese, and the Indian experience! We find here representatives from all the nations of Europe easily blending with each other. But we find elements that will not assimilate. The Negro, the Indian, and the Chinese, who do not belong to the same family, repel each other, and are repelled by the Europeans. "The antagonistic elements are in contact, but refuse to unite, and as yet no agent has been found sufficiently potent to reduce them to unity."

But the case with Americo-Liberians and the aborigines is quite different. We are all descendants of Africa. In Liberia there may be found persons of almost every tribe in West-Africa, from Senegal to Congo. And not only do we and the natives belong to the same race, but we are also of the same family.

---

* Macaulay's History of England, vol. I. chap. 1.

The two peoples can no more be kept from assimilating and blending than water can be kept from mingling with its kindred elements. The policy of Liberia is to diffuse among them as rapidly as possible the principles of Christianity and civilization, to prepare them to take an active part in the duties of the nationality which we are endeavoring to erect. Whence, then, comes the slander which represents Liberians as "maintaining a distance from the aborigines—a constant and uniform separation"?

To take part in the noble work in which they are engaged on that coast, the government and people of Liberia earnestly invite the descendants of Africa in this country.* In all our feebleness, we have already accomplished something; but very little in comparison of what has to be done. A beginning has been made, however — a great deal of preparatory work accomplished. And if the intelligent and enterprising colored people of this country would emigrate in large numbers, an important work would be done in a short time. And we know exactly the kind of work that would be done. We know that where now stand unbroken forests would spring up towns and villages, with their schools and churches — that the natives would be taught the arts of civilization — that their energies would be properly directed — that their prejudices would disappear — that there would be a rapid and important revulsion from the practices of heathenism, and a radical change in their social condition—

* The Legislature of Liberia, at its last session, 1861-62, passed an Act authorizing the appointment of Commissioners to "itinerate among and lecture to the people of color in the United States of North-America, to present to them the claims of Liberia, and its superior advantages as a desirable home for persons of African descent." The President appointed for this work, Professors Crummell and Blyden and J. D. Johnson, Esq.

that the glorious principles of a Christian civilization would diffuse themselves throughout those benighted communities. Oh! that our people would take this matter into serious consideration, and think of the great privilege of kindling in the depths of the moral and spiritual gloom of Africa a glorious light—of causing the wilderness and the solitary place to be glad—the desert to bloom and blossom as the rose—and the whole land to be converted into a garden of the Lord.

Liberia, then, appeals to the colored men of this country for assistance in the noble work which she has begun. She appeals to those who believe that the descendants of Africa live in the serious neglect of their duty if they fail to help to raise the land of their forefathers from her degradation. She appeals to those who believe that a well-established African nationality is the most direct and efficient means of securing respectability and independence for the African race. She appeals to those who believe that a rich and fertile country, like Africa, which has lain so long under the cheerless gloom of ignorance, should not be left any longer without the influence of Christian civilization—to those who deem it a far more glorious work to save extensive tracts of country from barbarism and continued degradation than to amass for themselves the means of individual comfort and aggrandizement—to those who believe that there was a providence in the deportation of our forefathers from the land of their birth, and that that same providence now points to a work in Africa to be done by us their descendants. Finally, Liberia appeals to all African patriots and Christians—to all lovers of order and refinement—to lovers of industry and enterprise—of peace, comfort, and happiness—to those who having felt the power of the Gospel in opening up to them life and immortality, are desirous that their benighted kindred should share in the same blessings. "Behold, the Lord thy God hath set the land before thee: go up and possess it, as the Lord God of thy fathers hath said unto thee; fear not, neither be discouraged."

INAUGURAL ADDRESS

AT THE

INAUGURATION OF LIBERIA COLLEGE,

AT MONROVIA,

JANUARY 23, 1862.

INAUGURAL ADDRESS.

Gentlemen of the Board of Trustees, and Respected Audience:

An old and venerable custom, existing in countries where colleges and universities have been long established, requires that he who is entering upon the responsible office of Professor, should publicly express the views which he entertains of the duties devolved upon him, and the manner in which he will discharge those duties. It is in accordance with this custom that I appear before you to-day.

This is an auspicious day for Liberia, and for West-Africa. The first College Edifice erected on this benighted shore has been completed; and we, descendants of Africa, are assembled to inaugurate it. Perhaps this very day, one century ago, some of our forefathers were being dragged to the hold of some miserable slaver, to enter upon those horrible sufferings of the "middle passage," preliminary to their introduction into scenes and associations of deeper woe. To-day, their descendants having escaped the fiery ordeal of oppression and slavery, and having returned to their ancestral home, are laying the foundation of intellectual empire, upon the very soil whence their fathers were torn, in their ignorance and degradation. Strange and mysterious providence!

It is among the most fortunate circumstances, connected with the founding of Liberia, that schools of a high order, and now a college, should be established in this early period of her history. It is impossible to maintain our national independence, or grow in the elements of national prosperity, unless the people are generally imbued with a proper sense of their duties and responsibilities, as citizens of a free government. The duties which devolve upon the citizens of Liberia, are as diversified and important as those which devolve upon citizens of larger nations and communities; and, in order to discharge those duties faithfully and successfully, we need all the fitness and qualification which citizens of larger nations possess. To say, as has been too often said, by persons abroad and by persons here, that the establishment of a college in Liberia at present is premature, is to set aside the experience of older countries, and to ignore the testimony which comes to us from a hundred communities far in advance of us, showing the indispensableness of institutions of a higher order, to send down, through all the ramifications of society, the streams of wholesome and elevating influence.

I regard this, then, as an auspicious day for Liberia; hoping that there will be such a feeling of appreciation, on the part of our people, of the importance of this Institution, and such active coöperation with it, as shall render it useful as a means of building us up in all those qualities which shall fit us for the discharge of our various duties, and draw towards us the attention and respect of the civilized world.

The fear need not be entertained that a course of study in this Institution will unfit men for the practical duties of life, render them proud, and distant, and haughty, and overbearing. Such is not the effect of a true education. I am aware that there prevails with some—and perhaps not entirely without foundation—the opinion that the effect of superior education is to inflate men and render them impracticable. There have been some among us who, not having trodden even the threshold of the temple of knowledge, have assumed an air of mysteriousness and profundity, in order to impress the multitude with their intellectual superiority and extraordinary importance. This is not, however, the legitimate effect of true knowledge. They are utter strangers to the genial influence of literature upon the social sentiments, who suppose that men must be distant, and haughty, and cold, in proportion as they are profound. The man who has really ascended Parnassus, does not encounter there, as on some Alpine summit, everlasting snows and ice, which chill and contract the heart. No; he finds himself in a warm and delightful atmosphere, which expands the heart, quickens the emotions, arouses the slumbering affections of the soul, and fits him for communication and communion with other minds; so that he experiences the greatest possible pleasure, in participating with others the benefits he enjoys. He does not, when he ascends the hill of science, find there luxuriant groves which allure him into ease and inactivity, where, like Tityrus,

"Patulæ recubans sub tegmine fagi,"

he might pass life away in quiet enjoyment. No; he has only reached a point from which he can contemplate the work to be done, and gather materials for carrying it on.

Every country has its peculiar circumstances and characteristics. So has Liberia. From this fact, it has often been argued that we need a peculiar kind of education; not so much colleges and high schools, as other means, which are more immediately and obviously connected with our progress. But to this we reply, that if we are a part of the human family, we have the same intellectual needs that other men have, and they must be supplied by the same means. It shows a painful ignorance of history, to consider the present state of things in Liberia as new and unprecedented, in such a sense as to render dispensable those most important and fundamental means of improvement, which other countries have enjoyed. Mind is every where the same; and every where it receives character and formation from the same elemental principles. If it have been properly formed and have received a substantial character, it will work out its own calling, solve its own problem, achieve its own destiny.

No country in the world needs, more than Liberia, to have mind properly directed. We are here isolated from the civilized world, and surrounded by a benighted people, with whom we are closely identified. And, in these circumstances, we are making the experiment, which, I venture to say, has never been made before, of establishing and maintaining a popular government, with a population, for the most part, of emancipated slaves. The government is thrown into the hands of the people, and they are called upon to give their opinions upon all subjects which can affect us as a nation; upon all the difficult subjects of finance, of legislation, and the most intricate points of constitutional law. Not only do they utter their opinions, but it is their right and privilege to act upon these opinions; and they do act upon them—with what success, alas! we are too well aware. And in addition to these political responsibilities, we have philanthropic duties to perform towards our aboriginal brethren—duties which require no little degree of intelligence and virtue.

De Tocqueville informs us that, before the colony that landed at Plymouth was as old as Liberia, there were laws enacted, establishing schools in every township, and obliging the inhabitants, under pain of heavy fines, to support them. Schools of a superior kind were founded in the same manner in the more populous districts. The municipal authorities were bound to enforce the sending of children to school by their parents.* It is certainly a very remarkable fact, that, in New-England, by the time the first child born in the colony had reached a proper age for admission to college, a college was established. They did not wait to have all those preparations, which some have fancied are necessary before Liberians can reap the benefit of a college. We are informed that the forests were yet standing; the Indian was still the near neighbor of the largest settlements; the colonists were yet dependent on the mother country for the very necessaries of life; and the very permanence of their settlements was as yet undecided, when they were erecting high schools and colleges. They did not regard it as too early to provide for the thorough education of their children. They had left their fatherland to seek an asylum of liberty on those distant shores, and they well knew that intelligence was indispensable to the enjoyment and maintenance of true liberty.

The people of the South were no less eager to provide themselves with the means of education. The colony of Virginia was still struggling against the difficulties and embarrassments incident to feeble settlements, when the first efforts were made by the inhabitants to

* *Democracy in America*, vol. I. chap. 7.

establish a college. As early as 1619, grants of land, and liberal subscriptions, were obtained for the endowment of the University of Henrico; and we may form some idea of the weak state of the colony, when we learn that the University was destroyed by an Indian massacre, and that the colony came very near being exterminated. Before the close of that century, however, the College of William and Mary was in successful operation.*

Why then should not Liberia, after forty years' existence, having secured the confidence and respect of the aboriginal tribes, enjoy the means of superior education? The name *College*, applied to this Institution, may seem ambitious; but it is not too early in our history for us to aim at such institutions. Of course we can not expect that it will at once fulfill all the conditions of colleges in advanced countries; but it may, in time, as many American colleges have done, grow into an Institution of respectability and extensive usefulness.

It can not be denied, that the studies which shall be pursued in this Institution are of great utility to this country just now. The college course will include all those studies by which a people's mind and heart are formed. We shall have the study of language in the most perfect forms in which it has ever been spoken by man — a study which, as we shall endeavor to show, aids greatly in the training and discipline of the mind.

We shall have the study of mathematics and physical science — which involves, of course, a study of the laws of nature, and the acquirement of the essential preliminary knowledge of all calculations, measurements and observations, on the sea and on the land.

We shall have — besides jurisprudence and interna-

---

* President Hale's Inaugural Address, Geneva College, 1855.

tional law — the study of intellectual and moral philosophy, by which is gained a knowledge of the mind, and the laws of thought, and of our duties to ourselves, to our fellow-men, to society, and to God.

Will any one of the studies, which I have enumerated, be superfluous in Liberia? So far from it, the course does not supply all our deficiencies.

But we need a *practical* education in Liberia. True; and so did the first settlers of North-America. And does not the college course supply such an education? What is a practical education? It is not simply preparing a person specially for any one sphere of life. It aims at practical results of a more important character — at imparting not simply skill in keeping accounts — in pleading at the bar — in surveying land — in navigating a vessel — but skill in exercising the intellect accurately and readily, upon any subject brought before it. The skill secured by a college education, is skill in the use of the mind.

The influence of the colleges planted in New-England, and elsewhere in the United States, in their early days, was most remarkable. "The eloquence nurtured at Harvard, rung like a trumpet-call, through town and forest, to rouse the quiet inhabitants to the revolutionary struggle; and the intelligence and learning which, starting from her classic shades, had been diffused through the whole community, had prepared all for understanding and discussing the principles of that liberty which belonged to them as men, and was guaranteed to them by the British constitution. Many of the lofty spirits of those times were taught to reason, and prepared to meet, in the discussion of the great questions at issue, the ablest counselors of the old world, and to maintain the cause of their country in the senate chamber—in these early institutions of learning. The success of that country in the struggle which made her free, as well as in commerce and the arts, has been owing to the unusual intelligence and virtue of her people—virtue, which could not have existed without intelligence, and was nourished by the same means—and intelligence, derived from her higher seats of learning, and diffused through her pulpits and her secondary schools, which, obtaining from the colleges educated teachers, shone with a borrowed but most salutary light upon the humblest cottages of the land."

As I remarked at the outset, the usage which brings me before you to-day, enjoins upon the speaker a topic which shall not be alien from the work in which he is to be engaged in the Institution. Allow me, therefore, to ask your kind attention, while I devote a portion of time to the consideration of the subject of LANGUAGE, and to setting forth the value and utility of the Latin and Greek languages, as means of education and culture.

I. Language is not natural to man. I mean that it did not originate with man. In common with other animals, man, as soon as he is born, can use the voice as a medium of communication, but only in a succession of cries; he can not articulate; he can not use language until he is taught, or until he acquires it by imitation. There is a diversity of opinion with regard to the origin of language; some supposing that the first man found himself suddenly endowed with the ability to give expression to his thoughts by oral sounds; while others maintain that, like all other attainments of man, language was made gradually. The latter opinion seems the more reasonable. We can not, from all we know of man, believe that this very important means of intercourse with his fellows—of conveying his thoughts, feelings, and experiences, to distant generations, was left to his invention, or to his precarious ingenuity. Man, left to himself, has never discovered any means of conveying his thoughts by articulate sounds. It is conclusively proved, that new-born babes, when left to themselves, or exposed among beasts, utter only sounds in imitation of those beasts.* The most natural way to man, of expressing his ideas, is by signs. This is the universal language. This is the only way that deaf mutes, who can not hear and imitate sounds, can convey their own and receive the impressions of others. Nearly all the travelers among the North-American Indians agree that they have ever had a language of signs, and can understand each other in this way, when they are unable to comprehend each other's speech; so that individuals of two far-distant Indian tribes, who understand not a word of each other's language, will intelligibly converse together, and contract engagements, without interpreters, "in such a surprising manner as is scarcely credible."

The infinite variety of languages which now so much impedes and incommodes the general intercourse of nations is the result of direct divine interposition. The whole earth, prior to the building of the tower of Babel, was "of one language, and of one speech;" but during the erection of that ambitious structure, the Lord "came down" and "confounded their language." Philologists have classified the various languages in groups, or families; but they seem reducible to one primitive idiom. "Every progress in the comparative study of languages, brings to light new analogies in the structure and in the grammatical forms and affinities of the roots

* *Bibliotheca Sacra*, vol. xviii. p. 775.

and terms; even the languages of the new continents do not seem to be excepted from this general resemblance." A distinguished American philologist beautifully says: "Nothing is found in the realms of speech, any more than in those of nature, 'without father or mother.' Here, as every where else, the maxim is true, 'Ex nihilo, nihil fit.' The languages, therefore, of the world, like the men who have spoken them, have all been bound together by a regular series of sequences, running link by link in luminous beauty, from any and every language now spoken upon earth, to the first language in which listening angels heard Adam and Eve discourse to each other; and from that back to God himself, the great All-in-all, from whose own girdle the golden chain of human speech divine was dropped lovingly down to man, in order to bind him to himself, and all nations in heavenly sympathy with each other."* Says Dr. Kalisch, an able Hebrew divine: "The linguistic researches of modern times have more and more confirmed the theory of one primitive Asiatic language, gradually developed into the various modifications by external agencies and influences. Formerly the Hebrew tongue was, by many scholars, advocated as the original idiom; for it was maintained both by early Jewish and Christian authorities, that as the race of Shem were no partners in the impious work of the Tower, they remained in possession of the first language, which the fathers of the earliest age had left to Noah; but this view, like the more recent one, that a child, if left alone, without human society, would speak Hebrew, is now classed among the popular errors."†

The greater number of scientific writers on language, agree that there was one primitive language, from which

* Dwight, *Bib. Sacra*, vol. xv. p. 404.
† *Historical and Critical Comment on Genesis*, chap. xi.

all the languages now spoken have sprung, and that that language was communicated to man by the Almighty. The question as to which language it was, is not quite settled; at present the probability inclines more to the Sanscrit.

II. Language is progressive. God did not, in other departments of his work, make at once full and complete manifestations; there was a gradual unfolding, according to circumstances, until there came to pass a full development. So we have every reason to believe it was with language. Man, in his primitive condition, did not possess all those mental states and wants which only age and experience could bring with them; he could not, therefore, have words to express what he had not seen, felt, or heard; nor could he form any conceptions, except from the things with which he was then in contact. When, therefore, the Divine Being assisted or instructed the first man to express by words his feelings, intentions, and thoughts, the instruction was adapted to his wants and circumstances. The simple forms of language which he then received, have been successively developed, and modified, and perfected, according as man has increased in the necessities and the arts of life. We find that among barbarous tribes, language is rude and deficient in point of words; so that the civilized foreigner, who wishes to convey his own ideas through the medium of such language, finds insuperable difficulties. Words are multiplied in proportion as the number of the ideas of a people is increased. Language "begins with the dawn of reflective consciousness, and unfolds itself as this becomes deeper and clearer."[*]

[*] Professor Shedd's Address on the *Relation of Language to Thought*.

Even in highly civilized countries, the vernacular, strictly speaking, or the language spoken by the masses, is very limited as to words, compared with the language of the educated. It is said that in England, the lower classes can not understand above one fourth part of that English which the higher classes speak. If any of the former visit the House of Lords, they sometimes sit with as much astonishment and disprofit, as if the debates were conducted in a new language. The vocabulary of terms used in the Houses of Parliament is one which is never pressed into the service of the common people.*

The character of the language spoken by any people is, therefore, a sure standard by which to judge of the attainments of that people in the arts of life. The poverty of the language of the ancient Britons, if we had no other proof of their extremely rude condition, would be enough to convince us that they had made very little progress in civilization. Even after the Saxon and Danish languages had been blended with each other, and with the aboriginal tongue, still the composite language had no "aptitude for all the highest purposes of the poet, the philosopher, and the orator," until it had been enriched by contributions from the languages of Greece and Rome. Take any of the leading English historians, Hume, Gibbon, Hallam, or Macaulay, and you will find that nearly three fourths of the words employed by them are of foreign origin; because there were no poets or philosophers, historians or orators, among the aboriginal inhabitants of that country. The language has progressed as the people have improved.

* Pycroft's *Ways and Words of Men of Letters*.

III. Language lies at the beginning and occupies an important place in the continuation of all human education. The child must first learn to understand language before he can receive ideas in any great number or variety; and he must learn to speak before he can express his wants. And when he grows up, if, in his early years, he has neglected the study of language, it matters not what progress or discoveries he may make in physical or mathematical science; before his knowledge can be made available, he must learn the use of language. This was the experience of George Stephenson, of railway notoriety, of Hugh Miller, and of others who, by force of "good, original brain," have arisen from a childhood of obscurity and poverty, to a useful and distinguished manhood.

The mastery of language, then, is a very important element in our qualification for usefulness. All our attainments would be useless, so far as accomplishing their true end is concerned, if we had no means of communion or communication with other minds. The true uses of knowledge are not to be found in centralization, but in distribution. And it is only by this distribution of our intellectual resources that we can enlarge them. Here also the scriptural assertion is verified: "There is that scattereth, and yet increaseth; there is that withholdeth more than is meet, and it tendeth to poverty." "Shut up within one's self, thought stagnates and knowledge decays." Language, therefore, as the instrument which an unerring Divinity has given to man for communicating thought and feeling, should be carefully studied and mastered, not only in its grammatical inflections and syntactical combinations, but in its original and derivative aspects.

As a means of thus mastering language, of understanding its genius and power, all the distinguished educators of modern times have chosen the study of the Greek and Latin languages. The Greek language is artistic and complete in its grammatical structure—a language of gracefulness and beauty, and highly adapted to æsthetic culture. The cultivation of the beautiful is one of the first steps towards civilization. The Greeks, who as a nation were the type of beauty, were an element in the development of mankind; and their language is indispensable to the opening of the mind for the reception and pursuit of abstract ideas. It was a language which the Romans assiduously studied, as a means of culture. The greatest orators and poets of Rome were cultivated by it. The famous advice of Horace will recur to the classical reader:

"Vos exemplaria Græca
Nocturnâ versate manu, versate diurnâ."*

The Latin language must be studied, not only for the disciplinary influence of the study upon the mind, but for its vast resources; its inward treasures, as well as its outward relations. It is connected with nearly all the languages of the past, and has contributed of its wealth to the formation of all the important modern languages. Its acquisition is really the key to a thorough knowledge of all the languages of the enlightened part of mankind.

The Latin and Greek languages have furnished all the linguistic culture, and have contributed to all the rich results of the higher education of the whole civilized world, for the last two thousand years. They who contemptuously speak of them as "dead" languages, know not that such utterances illustrate their own lack of culture. These languages *are* "dead" to them, in all

* Epistola ad Pisones, 268.

their inward beauty and force, and in all their outward scientific relations; they can no more appreciate them, than a blind man can appreciate the colors of the rainbow, or a deaf man the sweet concords of music. To men of high culture, however, these languages are still living, and their power is every day felt. Without a knowledge of them, no Englishman, Frenchman, Spaniard, or Italian, can thoroughly comprehend his own vernacular; whilst the man who has cultivated an acquaintance with them, is possessed of the elements of nearly all the languages of Southern Europe. Without the slightest acquaintance with the Italian language, he will feel at home in Italy. Before he has seen a French or Spanish grammar, or heard a Frenchman or Spaniard speak, he will be able to sit down and read, with some satisfaction, French and Spanish literature. Such is the influence of these "dead" languages upon the literature of the day.

The Greek and Latin languages must be studied by the English student, in order to a complete mastery of his own language. The English language is, for the most part, a derived language, secondary in its origin. "Into the English, as into the bosom of a great central sea, all the streams of the past and present have poured, and are still pouring their varied contents." To understand this language, thoroughly, then, we must give attention to those languages which have contributed most largely to its formation. Many persons who, not possessing a knowledge of these "dead" languages, suppose themselves to be very good English scholars, every day use words whose meaning they do not understand. They refer with great confidence to their English dictionaries as the ultimate standard, not knowing that even in the best dictionaries the etymological scholar discovers fatal deficiencies. The man who is entirely devoid of a knowledge of the Greek and Latin languages can never, generally speaking, use English words with skill or satisfaction to himself. He can not perceive, in the words which he uses, their original life and beauty. He can not, out of the very words themselves, give his reason for employing them in preference to others. He must be the slave of his dictionary; and all his lexicographical researches must be uncertain and unsatisfactory. No perfection of English scholarship can be acquired without a knowledge of the "dead" languages.

But there is a still higher reason for the study of these languages, and that is, the mental culture and discipline which they afford. No other means has yet been found to supply their place, for purposes of scholastic discipline. All the present culture of Europe, and the pure and elevated taste manifested by her best scholars, have been derived from the study of the Greek and Roman writers. After the lapse of centuries, those great masters of thought stand unrivaled in their peculiar sphere as the intellectual educators of mankind. To neglect them, is to shut ourselves out from delightful associations with the best minds. It is through them we have access to the most sacred places of thought, and enjoy the influence of those mighty conceptions which still control the literary world. It is through them that we are carried back to the youthful days of the world, and enjoy something of the freshness and vigor of those early times—the spring-time of human intellect. "Greece and Rome," to quote the eloquent language of Dr. Temple,* "have given us more than any results of discipline, in the never-dying memory of their fresh and youthful life. It is this, and not

* Head-Master of Rugby School.

only the greatness or the genius of the classical writers, which makes their literature preëminent above all others. There have been great poets, great historians, great philosophers, in modern days. Greece can show few poets equal, none superior to Shakspeare. Gibbon, in many respects, stands above all ancient historians. Bacon was as great a master of philosophy as Aristotle. Nor, again, are there wanting, great writers of times older, as well as of times later, than the Greek; as, for instance, the Hebrew prophets. But the classics possess a charm quite independent of genius. It is not their genius only which makes them attractive. It is the classic life, the life of the people of that day. It is the image there only to be seen, of our highest natural powers in their freshest vigor. It is the unattainable grace of the prime of manhood. It is the pervading sense of youthful beauty. Hence, while we have elsewhere great poems and great histories, we never find again that universal radiance of fresh life which makes even the most commonplace relics of classic days, models for our highest art. The common workman of those times breathed the atmosphere of the gods. What are now the ornaments of our museums, were then the every day furniture of sitting and sleeping-rooms. In the great monuments of their literature, we can taste this pure inspiration most largely; but even the most commonplace fragments of a classic writer, are steeped in the waters of the same fountain. Those who compare the moderns with the ancients, genius for genius, have no difficulty in claiming for the former, equality, if not victory. But the issue is mistaken. To combine the highest powers of intellect with the freshness of youth, was possible only once, and that is the glory of the classic nations."[*]

[*] "The Education of the World," in *Essays and Reviews*, 1861.

But it has been asked: "Why devote so much time to the study of those authors in their own language, when they have been so well and ably translated? Why undergo the labor to traverse the same ground which they passed over, to bring to us those hidden treasures? Why not use our time and strength in accomplishing something else?" We reply, that the road to learning can not be made royal. It is true that the present ever gathers into itself the results of the past; that the world is to-day what it is, as the result of the whole of its antecedents; that "we reap the fruits of the toil of the men of the earliest ages;" but this is true with regard to the race in the aggregate. The individual man must undergo an intellectual discipline, more or less severe, before he can be prepared to comprehend and to profit by the results of the past. The faculties of the child that is born to-day are essentially the same as those of the child born in the earliest period, and must be developed by a similar process, though there may be a vast difference in the ultimate development. Of all men of eminent abilities, in all ages, it may be said:

> "The eminence they reached and kept,
> Was not attained by sudden flight,
> But they, while their companions slept,
> Were toiling upwards in the night."

Every man must go over the same ground, experience the same toil, struggle with the same difficulties. No man, in any generation, is born with wings to enable him to soar to the lofty hights of literature or science. It is by "slow degrees, by more and more," that those "cloudy summits" are "scaled and climbed." And every man, as by painful efforts he ascends those eminences, may, from the boundless prospect and varied wealth, bring contributions to literature and science.

The discipline of mind which is secured from the study of the dead languages can not be obtained by the use of translations. They are the only languages which are developed according to the rules of perfect art; and no other language can fully supply their place. Besides the wholesome exercise which is derived from the weighing and balancing of the meaning of words, observing and preserving nice distinctions, there is the process of reasoning which must be employed in every effort to translate. The student who has read one or two leading Latin and Greek works, has not much more labor with the lexicon. What he needs now, in prosecuting the study of the classic authors, is "a clear head and close attention to the context."* The drudgery of "hunting up" every word in the lexicon, is ended; and he has reached a region of plodding, indeed, but of higher, intellectual plodding. Being able to select his own meaning for each word out of the word itself and its connections, he goes beyond the mere forms of words and sentences, to the principles they contain. He imbibes the spirit of the writer. His mind enlarges. He learns to form a correct estimate of the merits and defects of composition. His taste is quickened, purified, and elevated; and by being obliged to extend his vocabulary as widely as that of the author he translates, he necessarily becomes familiar with a number of new words, of which, perhaps, under other circumstances, he might only have heard. He thus acquires a command of language, and enters upon a course of indefinite improvement — a road that leads to the loftiest attainment.

And then the study of translations can not introduce us to a knowledge of the style and beauties of the clas-

* Macaulay's Essay on the Athenian Orators.

sic authors. We must become acquainted with them through the words they spoke and wrote, and the manner in which they spoke and wrote those words. It is true that the thoughts and opinions of Herodotus, Xenophon, and Demosthenes, of Cicero, Horace, and Tacitus, may be expressed in a translation. We may be able, by studying translations, to get something of the substance of the original. But of the peculiar character and spirit of the style of the writer; of those special qualities which belong to and are inseparable from the languages in which they wrote; of those associations which are often linked to a single word, and which no combination of English words can express—of all these things, we can get only an imperfect idea from the most exact translation. "The dead languages possess not merely a grammatical structure essentially unlike that of living languages, but a peculiar system of poetic symbols, which, often with one expression, open an entire gallery of pictures, that must be, almost invariably, lost in a translation."*

The experience of all the literary men in the world proves that the study of classical literature, as a means of intellectual culture, is highly important. But it must be pursued as a means, not as an end; not to make us expert in verbal criticisms, or for pedantic displays, but for the discipline of mind, which the perusal and contemplation of the great models impart; for the large, thoroughly genial, and generous scholarship which they bestow. Pursued in this way, the influence of classical literature can not fail to be beneficial. Sir Robert Peel, who won the first honors at the Oxford University, both in the classics and mathematics, declared that " by far the greater portion of the

* Bishop Esaias Tegnér.

chief names that have floated down on the stream of time, are those of men eminent for classical acquirements and classical tastes." "Take the Cambridge Calendar, for two hundred years," says Lord Macaulay, "look at the Church, the Parliament, or the Bar, and it has always been the case that the men who were first in the competition of the schools have been the first in the competition of life." All the distinguished scholars of Great Britain have been deeply imbued with classical learning. Curran, the Irish orator, carried his Virgil always in his pocket. Fox was devoted to the classics. Sheridan pored over Euripides by night and by day. Pitt is said to have been the best Greek scholar in England. Lord Brougham — himself a marvel of classical lore—in giving an account of the manner in which Robertson, the historian, studied composition, says: "Translations from the classics, and especially from the Greek, of which he was a perfect master, formed a considerable part of his labor. He considered this exercise as well calculated to give an accurate knowledge of our own language, by obliging us to weigh the shades of difference between words or phrases, and to find the expression, whether by the selection of the terms or the turning of the idiom, which is required for a given meaning."* The same distinguished nobleman gives the following advice — the result of his own rich and varied experience — to a young student:

"If he would be a great orator, he must go at once to the fountain-head, and be familiar with every one of the great orations of Demosthenes. His taste will improve every time he reads and repeats to himself, (for he should have the fine passages by heart,) and he will learn how much may be done by a skillful use of a few words, and a rigorous rejection of superfluities. In this view, I hold a familiar knowledge of Dante to be next to Demosthe-

* *Lives of Men of Letters and Science.*

nes. It is in vain to say that imitations of these models won't do for our times. First, I do not counsel any imitation, but only an imbibing of the same spirit. Secondly, I know from experience, that nothing is half so successful in these times, (bad though they be,) as what has been formed on the Greek models. I use a very poor instance in giving my own experience, but I do assure you, that both in courts of law and Parliament, and even to mobs, I have never made so much play, (to use a very modern phrase,) as when I was almost translating from the Greek. I composed the peroration of my speech for the Queen in the Lords, after reading and repeating Demosthenes for three or four weeks, and I composed it twenty times over at least, and it certainly succeeded in a very extraordinary degree, and far above any merits of its own."*

But it is objected to these classical pursuits, that these are practical times, and the facilities for practical information are so multitudinous that it is far more profitable for the purposes of life to devote attention to the exuberance and diversity of knowledge to be found in the innumerable newspapers and periodicals of the day than to waste time in poring over the relics of antiquity; that, in these days, when the prodigious powers of the press are developed in the regular and unceasing issue of pamphlets and tracts, works in series and light literature, men might dispense with every other means of improvement and instruction. "Why need we go up to knowledge when knowledge comes down to us?" To this we reply once more, that culture must be attained by the same means by which it has always been attained. Every man, before he can be fitted for the more important intellectual achievements, must tread the highway of hard work and laborious practice. The mind must first be formed before it can be filled to advantage. Our real improvement depends not so much upon the quantity as upon the quality of what the mind takes in, and upon the manner in which

---

* Letter to Zachary Macaulay, in 1823, with reference to his son, Thomas Babington Macaulay, the historian, then at Cambridge.

it is taken in. Lord Macaulay tells us, that "Rumford proposed to the Elector of Bavaria a scheme for feeding his soldiers at a much cheaper rate than formerly. His plan was simply to compel them to masticate their food thoroughly. A small quantity thus eaten, according to that famous projector, affords more sustenance than a large meal hastily devoured."* Thus it is with the mind; not the cramming, but the mastication and the digestion secure the nutriment. A man may constantly devour all the periodicals and newspapers, as they are daily issued throughout the world, and after he has gathered all the information they contain, may not be as well prepared for usefulness and efficiency in the world of letters as the man who has patiently given his time and attention to one or two of the great masters in the language in which they wrote. Some of the great English writers devoted nearly all their time to the study of one or two of the classic authors. A learned and distinguished English nobleman carried his admiration of one of them so far as to exclaim:

> "Read Homer once, and you can read no more;
> For all books else appear so mean, so poor,
> Verse will seem prose; but still persist to read,
> And Homer will be all the books you need."*

The classics have been tried for centuries; their value and utility have often been denied, but they have as often been successfully defended; so that now, in the literary world, there is all but a unanimous decision in their favor.

The friends of education in Liberia have long desired to see the same means of intellectual culture which other countries have enjoyed, possessed by Liberians;

---
* *Essay on the Athenian Orators.*
* *Preface to Pope's Translation of the Iliad.*

and as a result of their efforts to secure for us these advantages, we have this College. Mind here, as we have said, is as mind elsewhere. We must rise, and we can rise by the same means by which other people have risen.

By the direction of Divine Providence, a momentous experiment has been committed to our hands on these benighted shores, an experiment in which are involved, to a great extent, the interests of Africa and the African race. Our responsibility in this land is a serious one. Sometimes we are appalled when we observe the fatal facility with which every form of social, moral, and political error from abroad takes root among us; when we see the readiness and eagerness with which some lay hold of the follies and nonsense which advanced communities are endeavoring to throw off. But let our hearts be cheered in view of the increase among us of those means which will counteract this facile disposition. We trust that by the encouragement and generous cultivation of literature, the public mind shall be directed to high principles and objects worthy of attainment.

Before we can realize all that greatness which we sometimes hear predicted in our public orations and speeches, we must avail ourselves of all those means by which a nation's heart is chastened, purified, and refined. We can not expect any special providential interference in our behalf to cause us to glide unconsciously into distinction and respectability. If we desire among us great poets, statesmen, and philosophers, if we would have profound theologians and able lawyers, we must resort to such books as the great men whose language we speak studied; to such books as Milton and Cowper, Bacon and Newton, Butler and Paley, studied; to the books which the great men of England *now* study; to the literary companions of Brougham, Gladstone, and D'Israeli; to Cæsar, Horace, and Tacitus; to Demosthenes and Cicero; to the Æneid, the Odyssey, and the Iliad. We may not expect to despise these and reap the fruits which are to be gathered only from them. "Till we have discovered some intellectual daguerreotype which takes off the course of thought, and the form, lineaments, and features of truth, as completely and minutely as the optical instrument produces the sensible object, we must come to the teachers of wisdom to learn wisdom; we must repair to the fountain and drink there."*

If we assiduously use the means of culture, we need not fear the results. We shall soon rise to a respectable if not a commanding position in the world of letters. Though much has been already done, there is yet a great deal to be achieved in the field of science and literature; and may we make no achievements? Let us hope that though civilization is well begun, even our feeble hands may shape its course; and that here on these benighted shores there may be elaborated noble principles out of which shall spring a practice that shall be exemplary to the whole civilized world.

Let us then encourage and sustain this Institution, that its influence may go forth into all the land. We can not expect that every child will attend college, but we may reasonably hope that such an influence will be sent forth from this Institution, and others that may hereafter be established, that those children who are not themselves able to attend college, may enjoy the benefit of the influence and tuition of those who have attended. Thus a higher tone of intellect will spread

* *Office and Work of Universities.*—J. H. Newman.

itself throughout all classes of society; and high and low, rich and poor, all uniting in the one great cause of Africa's redemption, we shall advance to national usefulness and respectability.

I feel the responsibility of the position I am assuming in connection with this Institution. I feel it for various reasons, many of which can be appreciated by you without any specific reference. I enter upon these duties with great diffidence, feeling that, while it is an honorable distinction, it will continue so only so long as he who fills it "acts well his part." I enter upon them, however, with confidence that, with the blessing of God, all that we or our friends abroad desire, can be accomplished. The liberality which conceived the idea of founding this Institution, and which, under various discouragements, persisted in carrying out that idea, will, we may hope, be continued towards us. In view of that liberal support which we may reasonably hope the Institution will receive from its friends in the United States; and in view of the feelings so manifest among Liberians to do all they can in behalf of the Institution, we may feel that the College opens this day under favorable auguries.

As a race we have been quite unfortunate. We have no pleasing antecedents—nothing in the past to inspire us. All behind us is dark, and gloomy, and repulsive. All our agreeable associations are connected with the future. When other people speak of glorious reminiscences and recollections, we must speak of glorious hopes and expectations. Let us then strive to achieve a glorious future.

"Let the dead Past bury its dead."

Let us devote ourselves to all those pursuits, success

in which will prove our brotherhood with the enlightened world. It is, after all, the mind and heart which prove the unity of the human races. The inward resemblance is far more forcible than outward disparities. We should not content ourselves with simply declaiming about our equality with the advanced races. Let our reply to the slanders of our enemies be a practical one. It is evident that it is only those who do not know us, except under the most unfavorable circumstances, who speak disparagingly of us. Judging from the specialities of their own limited experience, they say that we are not susceptible of the same progress; that we can not achieve in science, literature, or art, what they can. It would not be wisdom in us to assail and abuse them for this, or to indulge in empty declamations about our ability. Let us, under any and all circumstances, prove to them that we can achieve just what they can, under similar circumstances — prove it practically. In works on logic, the sophistical argument is often introduced to prove that motion is impossible; and it is usual, before handling it according to logical rules, to suggest a practical refutation of it — *solvitur ambulando*. Such is the reply which we should strive to make to those whose interest it has been, and now is, to throw discredit upon us.

It is very true that there must be the struggle and perseverance of many years before the associations of our oppressed condition in the Western hemisphere, with all their train of obloquies and prejudices, shall be obliterated. But our case is not unprecedented. All peoples who have risen from obscurity have had the same opposition of contempt to contend against. A few centuries ago the name of Briton was disdained by the Romans; and later still, the name of Englishman, which is now being carried down on such a tide of glory to distant ages, was the object of the impetuous contempt of the proud Norman.* Let us think of this when our adversaries bring their names, and their influence, and their arguments to bear against us. And when they pour their indignities, and fasten their disgraceful epithets upon us, let us take comfort in the thought that we are now beginning to enjoy the means which their ancestors were obliged to possess before they could rise from their obscure, ignoble, and ignorant condition.

Many of our adversaries are not ashamed to aver that no change of our circumstances will avail to release their understanding from the influence of its old associations. But such assertions are the result of a narrow view of things. We believe that, notwithstanding all their perverse representations of us — all their spiteful malignity — all their pretended immovable hardness — all the inveteracy of their prejudice — they will not be able to withstand demonstrations of superior ability, furnished by a successful pursuit of science, literature, and art.

But we must acknowledge that there are adverse influences, arising from our peculiar circumstances, isolation from the civilized world, difficulty of procuring books and other means of culture. We must, therefore, nerve ourselves for the arduous work that lies before us. Our struggle must be the harder and more strenuous, in proportion to the unyielding influence of the force by which we are opposed. The struggle may be long, but let us persevere. The road to greatness, whether individual or national, is no " primrose path of dalliance."

The first College in West-Africa is founded. Lord

---

* See Macaulay's *History of England*, vol. I. chap. I.

Macaulay's prediction, uttered forty years ago, of the illustrious University at Timbuctoo,* though uttered jocosely, is receiving realization. Truth is proving itself stranger than fiction. We hail this Institution as the precursor of incalculable blessings to this benighted land — as the harbinger of a bright and happy future for science, literature, and art, and for all the noblest interests of the African race.

* In a very humorous and entertaining article, styled "A prophetic account of an Epic Poem, to be published in 2824," Lord Macaulay predicts that in that year there will exist at Timbuctoo — established how long previously he does not say — an illustrious University, to which all the ingenuous youths of every country will be attracted by the high scientific character and eminent literary attainments of its Professors.—*Miscellaneous Writings*, vol. I. p. 142.

A EULOGY

PRONOUNCED ON

REV. JOHN DAY,

SUPERINTENDENT OF THE MISSIONS OF THE SOUTHERN BAPTIST CONVENTION IN WEST-AFRICA, AND CHIEF-JUSTICE OF THE REPUBLIC OF LIBERIA.

BEFORE THE CITIZENS OF MONROVIA,

IN THE PROVIDENCE BAPTIST CHURCH,

ON THE EVENING OF MARCH 3d, 1859.

Nudaeque Veritas quando aliam invenict parem?—Non.

A Eulogy Pronounced on Reb. John Day.

There are times in the history of nations as of individuals, when they are called upon by the voice of Providence to look back upon their past, to examine their present, and to endeavor to rectify whatever is wrong, to adjust whatever is disordered, and to harmonize whatever is discordant in their social and political organization, to see whether they have not departed too far from the old landmarks, or whether, destitute of an experience sufficient for a wise eclecticism, they have not adopted principles which militate against their progress and success. And, perhaps, no occasion more naturally suggests this retrospection and introspection than when called upon, as we are called upon this evening, to recite the history and reproduce the examples of those who have occupied positions of trust and responsibility, who have made themselves useful to the community; by whose wisdom, patriotism, and energy the nation has been advanced in respectability and prosperity, but who, by the rude entrance of death, have been torn from our embraces.

And, perhaps, there never was a time in the history of Liberia when we needed more carefully to ponder our condition; when the necessity seemed greater to hold up to our view whatever was virtuous and exemplary in the character of our fathers; that by summoning to our gaze, from those pure and lofty regions, their noble spirits, there may possibly be disposted from the midst of us that selfishness and unpatriotic feeling, and that spirit of disunion which we fear are taking the place of the public spirit, the enlarged benevolence, the self-sacrificing zeal, and the spirit of unity, under the influence of which this nation was founded, and by the aid of which it has been brought thus far.

The history of the late Rev. John Day, which we now purpose briefly to review, is not, it is true, marked by any of those stirring incidents, those marvelous and exciting adventures, those heroic actions which are pleasing to the minds of some. He achieved no great and remarkable exploits, which by the common and voluntary consent of mankind, place his name at once high among the great and honored of the earth. But there are, nevertheless, points in his history, monotonous and undiversified as a history enacted for the most part in Liberia must of necessity be, from the consideration of which important lessons may be gathered. We shall attempt, therefore, on this occasion, to collect some of the materials, which render his memory dear to every Liberian, to every Christian, and which should dispose us to cherish that memory as a precious inheritance, and to transmit it as a valuable legacy to future generations.

John Day was born in the northern part of the State of North-Carolina, in the year 1797. His native county, bordering upon the State of Virginia, was influenced not a little by the manners and customs of Virginian life. The circumstances of his birth were favorable. Born of a family of a high degree of respectability and held in great esteem by their white neighbors, his privileges were superior to those of many of his race in that country. And in the region where he was born and brought up, as indeed over the greater portion of North-Carolina and Virginia at that time, the distinction which now prevails between respectable persons of color and white persons was not known. Nathaniel Turner had not yet achieved his magnificent failure, and abolitionism had not yet assumed its rabid and sectional character. In his youthful education Mr. Day was fortunate. He attended the best schools in the county, and sat side by side with the sons of the most aristocratic planters. He was born at a time when the spirit that engendered the American Revolution was still rife among the people; when the exciting oratory of Patrick Henry still rang in their ears; when the mighty reverberations of his "Give me liberty, or give me death!" had not yet died from the mountain-ranges of Old Virginia. Sentiments averse to oppression of every kind still pervaded the breasts of the white inhabitants, and were diffused throughout their conversation. Mr. Day, allowed freely to mingle with the immediate descendants of the Jeffersons, the Randolphs, the Henrys, caught the flame of liberty and independence. And, as he looked around, and saw the majority of his brethren in a thralldom, which, by that keen foresight with which he was gifted, he saw would sooner or later affect unfavorably the condition of all persons of color, he sighed for a land where he might not witness the degradation of his brethren. He thought of Hayti, but he thought also of its foreign language, its priestcraft, and its frequent revolutions. He formed various plans for his future life, looking forward to a time when, amid some fortunate scene, and beneath some auspicious sky, he would realize his ardent desires for the enjoyment of liberty untrammeled by the adventitious circumstance of color.

Having been put to the trade of cabinet-making, he made such proficiency in that branch of industry that he was soon enabled to establish himself in business. By the superior finish and strength of his work, he attracted considerable custom. The most distinguished persons for miles around furnished him with work. He soon made himself a competency. But just as he was forming plans large and magnificent for his worldly aggrandizement and gratification, just as he was beginning to say with the rich man of old, "My grounds have brought forth plentifully, what shall I do?" it pleased the Great Head of the Church, by that mysterious influence whose operation is like the wind, blowing where it listeth, to transform his moral nature and make him a child of God. He found himself, to use his own words when relating the wonderful transition, in a new world. He found himself with new feelings and new desires, new predilections and new antipathies. He must now, therefore, form new plans. He looked abroad upon the world, and his enlarged heart took in all mankind. He felt that he had a work to do. He felt that it was his duty, as he esteemed it his privilege, to exhort others to flee from that impending wrath from which as a brand from the everlasting burnings he had been plucked. He was strongly impressed with the conviction that he should devote himself to the important business of preaching the Gospel. Having enjoyed the advantages of a good English education, he entered, through the recommendation of some friend, a theological class, whose reading was directed by Rev. Mr. Clopton, a Baptist minister of profound learning, skillful in the languages, and an adept in metaphysical science. Standing foremost in the ranks of Baptist ministers at that time, Mr. Clopton was eminently fitted for the duties of preparing young men for the ministry. Rev. Dr. J. B. Jeter, of Richmond, Virginia, then quite a young man, also frequented Mr. Clopton's study. Mr. Clopton had paid close attention to the laws of the mind, and had great facility in explaining difficulties in religious experience, which at that time frequently troubled Mr. Day. And from him, doubtless, the subject of our remarks acquired that love for metaphysical discussion and research which those who were intimate with him, or attended his preaching, could not fail to discover.

While pursuing his studies under Mr. Clopton, the colony of Liberia, as an asylum for free persons of color, began to attract attention in that part of the country where he resided. No sooner had he heard of the place than he at once made up his mind to cast in his lot with the people who, on these far-off shores, and in this insalubrious clime, were endeavoring to establish a home for themselves and their children. Coincident with the desire for a land of liberty, there was now a burning zeal to preach the Gospel to the thousands of degraded Africans who roam these forests. He diligently applied himself to the work of preparation for the Gospel ministry. But unfortunately for the intellectual advancement of Mr. Day, a circumstance transpired—a circumstance to which, even down to the day of his death, he frequently referred with expressions of unmingled regret—which obliged him to relinquish his studies before he had gone through the prescribed course, and enter upon the active duties of the calling which he had chosen.

Having sacrificed his property, he embarked in December of the year 1830, with a most amiable wife, and four interesting children, for this land, which was so soon to be the grave of the affectionate group. He arrived in Liberia, entered at once upon his sacred duties, pursuing the business of cabinet-making for his support, and preaching as often as opportunity offered. He had not been long in the land before he saw his lovely companion stricken down by the relentless hand of death— a companion to whose charms and loveliness he was most keenly alive, and around whom the most ardent affections of his soul were so firmly entwined, that the great depths of his heart seemed upheaved by the severance. Then, one after another, he saw his beloved offspring wrapped in the chilling embraces of the grim monster, and conveyed to the house appointed for all living, until his whole family melted away from him, and none was left to remind him of the scenes and associations of the past. There he stood all alone in a new country, amid new scenes and associations; there he stood, like some solitary oak in the dead of winter, stripped of its foliage, and exposed, dry and defenseless, to all the beatings of the northern storms. Finding himself in this grievous solitude, and entirely at a loss how to dispose of the sad and weary hours that hung so oppressively upon him, he abandoned himself to gloomy abstractions and melancholy reveries. This led to the supposition that there was some unhingement of his mental organization. But notwithstanding his deep afflictions he never murmured; was never disposed to abandon the field which he had chosen for the labors of his life. He had numerous inducements to return to the land of his birth. His relatives, in comfortable and respectable circumstances, urged him again and again to return. Several wealthy friends anxiously waited to welcome him. But he had put his hand to the plow, and he would not look back. His ardent and cherished desire was to labor for the evangelization of his heathen brethren in this land, and he would not, notwithstanding his deep bereavements, and the imminent danger in which his own life often stood, swerve from his noble purpose. Here we have an instance of the triumph of grace in the soul. Here we see true Christian benevolence, the constraining love of Christ, the new, living, and all-controlling principle implanted in every regenerate heart, rising superior to all earthly interests, forsaking father and mother, and hazarding life itself for the cause of Christ. Oh! in the heart of the Christian a deep and everflowing fountain has been opened, flowing out to all the world. "There is not the wreck of humanity it will not pity; there is not an infected prison it will not enter; there is not a pestilential climate or an inhospitable region it will not visit; there is no peril of robbers, nor peril of the sea, nor peril of false brethren, nor hunger, nor thirst it will not hazard in behalf of human redemption."

After Mr. Day had resided here for several years, a mission was established by the Northern Baptist Board of Missions, with which he became connected, and in the service of which, for a number of years, he was abundant in labors. The principal seat of the operations of that Board was in the county of Grand Bassa. Frequently have we sat and heard him recite for hours together the interesting and instructive incidents of those laborious, painful, and hazardous tours which he repeatedly made for hundreds of miles into the interior, preaching and teaching the people. And there are now to be found scattered all over that country delightful fruits of his labors. Taking the city of Buchanan as a center, and with a radius of sixty or seventy miles, describe a semicircle, and there is no point to which you can go within that semicircle where the name of John

Day is not a household word, and at many points you will readily recognize precious evidences of his toils and efforts.

Mr. Day subsequently became connected with the Southern Baptist Convention, who have established missions throughout Liberia, at Sierra Leone, and in Central Africa. For several years, and up to the hour of his death, he filled the responsible position of superintendent of their missions in Liberia and at Sierra Leone, and prosecuted to the utmost of his ability the arduous duties of that station of trust.

But Mr. Day *was patriotic.* Of this no citizen of Liberia, within the sound of my voice, needs any elaborate demonstration. Residing within the limits and being a citizen of a nation in the incipient stages of progress, he felt that, notwithstanding his arduous ministerial labors, he had a work to perform in shaping the political institutions of his country. No love of indulgence or ease, no dread of severe application, kept him from striving to qualify himself for usefulness to his country and fellow-citizens. He studied closely and patiently the science of jurisprudence and the general principles of statesmanship, so that he was fitted for usefulness in all those positions for which intelligent men are needed in rising communities. Nor were his talents and acquirements slighted by his fellow-citizens. After having filled various subordinate offices, elective and otherwise, he was, in the year 1853, placed as successor of Chief-Justice Benedict at the head of the Judiciary, which position he occupied with dignity and credit until his demise. It is said by competent judges that his charges to juries and decisions, when Judge of the Court of Quarter Sessions in the county of Grand Bassa, were most elaborate, and discovered a deep insight into legal principles. In the Legislative hall he did not very often take the floor, but whenever he did his counsels were wise and judicious. His remarks were brief, but to the point. And when he occupied leading positions on committees, where important reports and other documents had to be prepared, he showed his wisdom and skill, did justice to his subject and credit to himself.

The declaration of the Independence of Liberia, the establishment of the first Republican government on the Western Shores of Africa, did not, it is true, solve any intricate problem in the history of nations. It did not shed any new light upon mankind with reference to the science of government. It was not the result of the elaboration of any novel principle in politics. But it poured new vigor into the poor, dying existence of the African all over the world. It opened a door of hope for a race long the doomed victims of oppression. It animated colored men every where to fresh endeavors to *prove* themselves men. It gave the example of a portion of this despised race, far away in the midst of heathenism and barbarism, under the most unfavorable circumstances, assuming the responsibilities, and coming forward into the ranks, of nations; and it demonstrated that, notwithstanding the oppression of ages, the energies of the race had not been entirely emasculated, but were still sufficient to establish and to maintain a nationality.

When the idea of bringing to pass this mighty achievement in the history of the race was first mooted, many regarded it as chimerical, some viewed it as presumptuous, and others thought it but little less than treason. In the county in which Mr. Day then resided there was considerable opposition to the measure; but, deeply thoughtful, he saw the beneficial results which were likely to accrue to the country and to the race from the assumption of Independence. He boldly advocated the measure, notwithstanding various threats from an exasperated populace. The boisterousness of the mob could not daunt him. He persevered, and rode triumphantly over the tumultuous surges. He was elected a delegate to the National Convention which assembled in this city to draft a Declaration of Independence and a Constitution for the new Republic. He was therefore among the signers of the Declaration of Independence. And here we are reminded of the melancholy fact that those distinguished men are fast passing away. One after another has entered upon his voyage to that

"——undiscovered country
From whose bourn no traveler returns."

But four of the twelve who sat in that memorable convention survive. This admonishes those of us who are youthful that soon the fathers will have gone forever, and it presses home to our hearts, with all the solemnity of the grave, the question: Are we preparing ourselves, by mental and moral culture, to take their places and lead on this infant nation, which they have established in weakness and in much trembling, to independence and glory?

Just at this point we trust we shall be excused if we digress for a few minutes. We have with regret noticed of late a growing tendency among some of the juvenile members of the community to depreciate the labors of our fathers, the pioneers of Liberia. We say with regret, because we conceive such a spirit to be in violation of the command, recorded in broad and solemn characters on the pages of God's Holy Book: "Honor thy father and thy mother *that thy days may be long upon the land which the Lord thy God giveth thee.*" We regret it because it is doing great injustice to the heroic men who for years have struggled, in sickness and in health, in joy and in sorrow, to maintain themselves on these shores. We are tauntingly asked: "What have these men done?" And we are told that "all that has been achieved has been achieved by foreign means." What have they done? We would ask in return, what have they *not* done? They have voluntarily expatriated themselves from the land of their birth; forsook the endearing scenes and associations of childhood; severed themselves from the comforts and conveniences of an advanced state of society; denied themselves the enjoyment of health, the pleasure of civilized and enlightened influences, and gave themselves up to a living death on these barbarous shores. And for what purpose? That they might found a home not for themselves, for they knew they would not live to enjoy it, but for us their posterity. Foreign means indeed! It is true they were poor men. They had no gold and silver to lavish out upon improvements; but mark their superior self-abnegation and heroism, *they gave themselves.* And what could foreign learning and foreign wealth have done without their groans, and sweat, and blood? Yes, they suffered keenly, and bore up heroically under their sufferings for us. Their work consisted in patient endurance — a task far more difficult than active exertion. Let us not, then, depreciate their sacrifices and toils, but rather let us endeavor to qualify ourselves to carry on, by labor and well-directed effort, what they have begun in intense suffering and endurance. And if we are wise to detect any faults or deficiencies in any of their doings, let us not boastingly expatiate upon them, but rather let us, taking the mantle of charity, hasten to spread it over them, lest, while we luxuriate and delight ourselves with ideas of our own superiority to them, there come over the land a physical barrenness, a mental and moral blight, because we have not accorded the reverence due to our fathers.

We are not by any means, however, asserting that it is incumbent upon us to entertain such unquestioning deference to the opinions and actions of our fathers as to reënact their errors, and proceed, right or wrong, in the beaten track; but we are for interring with their bones the ill they may have done, encouraging the vitality of their virtuous deeds, and immortalizing their exemplary conduct. Let us emulate their noble actions. Let us not be content to live and die without doing something to ameliorate the condition of our downtrodden race. Oh! let us not be drones in the great hive of humanity.

> "In the world's broad field of battle,
> In the bivouac of life,
> Be not like dumb, driven cattle,
> Be ye heroes in the strife."

But we must return from our digression. Not only was Mr. Day laborious and diligent in qualifying himself for the public duties which he was so frequently called upon to perform, but he assiduously endeavored to fit himself for usefulness in the more private scenes of life. In that part of Liberia where he spent the greater portion of his time, there was seldom any physician, yet there were frequently cases among the people which needed medical attention. Mr. Day, therefore, gave himself, in addition to his numerous other studies, to the reading of medical works, and to the study of the natural sciences, that he might fit himself for ordinary practice. He soon acquired a sufficient knowledge of pathological principles and of therapeutics to enable him to be a very useful practitioner among the poor of his neighborhood. He willingly went from house to house, administering relief to the sick, healing the diseases of the body, and endeavoring to bind up the wounds of the spirit. Not a little of his earnings was expended in unwearied services among the poor and afflicted. By his well-bred gentility, the cordiality of his manners, and his sympathy with their griefs, he won the esteem and love of all around him. The sick and the afflicted, the poor and needy, were satisfied that he was their friend; and in the very humblest of their tenements he was met with exhibitions of their warmest welcome. In these private and retired acts, we have the most complete demonstration of the greatness of his spirit.

> "The drying of a single tear has more
> Of honest fame than shedding seas of gore."

We make a great mistake when we confine deeds of eminence to public scenes and magnificent occasions. It is often in the loneliness of a limited social or domestic circle, and in the discharge of the most commonplace duty, that the greatest self-denial has to be exercised. Men in obscure stations, of whom the world never hears, may have the hardest tasks to perform, and the greatest sacrifices to make, in the cause of God and religion. We should not lavish all our applause and admiration on such as stand foremost in the ranks of philanthropists, and whose names stand prominently forth as having done and suffered much to alleviate human suffering. We should not confine the honors of a true philanthropy to those who, in the sight and amid the applauses of thousands, pour out of their abundance in the cause of charity. We conceive that he who, sequestered from the gaze of the multitude, "little and unknown," distributes daily and habitually of his earnings to satisfy the needs of an indigent neighborhood, is to the full as deserving as he whose thousands, abstracted from a large and constantly increasing heap, are bestowed in the vicinity of a newspaper-office.

Mr. Day, then, by his activity in the performance of those deeds of charity, which were far removed from the observation of men generally, which attracted no attention, showed that he was possessor of a large and expansive soul; and though he did not attain to the celebrity of a Howard, he was none the less deserving of it, on the principle inculcated by our Saviour himself: "He that is faithful in that which is least is faithful also in much."

Mr. Day was also a soldier of no ordinary courage. His country never called for his services in that capacity but he was ready to respond; and when he believed that duty required it, he would brave the greatest dangers. On several occasions has he risked his life among uncounted numbers of the enemy, accompanied only by a few men, others refusing to follow, regarding his undertakings from their very boldness as the result of some mental disorder. Nothing intimidated him from any position to which he believed himself invited by the interests of his country.

But it is especially as a Christian and a Christian minister that we delight to contemplate Mr. Day. Believing himself called to the responsible work of preaching the Gospel, he devoted himself to it for more than thirty years with unremitting diligence. Although he had not received any of the honorary distinctions of literary institutions, although he was no graduate of any Theological Seminary, he had made great proficiency in the sublime science of Theology. He had carefully studied all the standard theological works of his own church and of several other denominations, so that on all theological subjects he was generally and perfectly at home.

Of his Christian character, what can we say that is not already known to you? You could not have met him at all if you do not agree that he had very high and very noble qualities. No one could have intercourse with him without perceiving prominent and interesting features in his character—features formed by the combination of virtue, courage, assiduity, diligence, perseverance, with natural talents and genius of no inferior order. There was such a frankness and sincerity in his words and actions, that no one could for a moment suppose that he was not what he seemed to be. What he said he meant. And whenever he made a promise he could be depended upon for its fulfillment, even though such fulfillment involved his own injury.

There was in his whole life a beautiful consistency and harmony. Not that we would claim for him an exemption from faults and errors. Such is poor human nature, that not unfrequently we find some of the highest qualities of mind and heart accompanied with very great defects. There were occasionally prominent in Mr. Day certain oddities of character; but these, if faults at all, were, to say the most of them, venial faults, when we consider the remarkable excellencies by which they were counterbalanced. On the disk of that bright luminary shining above us, the glorious king of day, may be discovered dark spots. But who would be accounted wise that should deny himself the privilege and pleasure of enjoying the benign rays of that "greater light," and employ his precious time in pointing out and counting the spots on the sun? Mr. Day had his defects, but the number, and strength, and vitality of his constitutional gifts and Christian graces, completely overshadowed those defects; they were scarcely seen, or, if seen, were but little regarded except by those whose moral vision was jaundiced by prejudice.

His piety was genuine. He had clear and distinct apprehensions of the great truths of salvation. He had a thorough persuasion that the promises of God recorded in the Bible are yea and Amen, in Christ Jesus. And there were no prophecies or promises upon which he more delighted to dwell than upon those which referred to Africa. He had strong faith in the assurance that "Ethiopia shall soon stretch out her hands unto God," and to hasten the fulfillment of this glorious promise he prayed and labored. It was a cherished desire of his to have extensive and permanent missions established by the Baptist Board among the natives throughout Liberia. And we could wish that this noble desire may be speedily realized, not only with respect to his own denomination, but all other denominations in Liberia. We trust that the death of this man of God will prove a stimulus to the "sacramental host of God's elect" to go up and possess the land. We trust that there may be generated in us a more enlarged benevolence, a more ardent zeal, and a more self-denying spirit, that, bravely closing up the vacancy which has just been occasioned in the ranks by the fall of a veteran, we may rally up with redoubled energy and power, determined to conquer or to die.

As a pastor of the Providence Baptist Church, so far as the weakness and infirmities of declining years permitted, he was faithful. For his pulpit ministrations he always made laborious preparation.

Crude and superficial views of truth never satisfied him. He followed closely the advice of the Apostle in giving attendance to reading, to exhortation, to doctrine. His discourses were the product of much thought and severe mental application. And he not unfrequently, with characteristic humility, referred to the intense labor which it cost him to prepare a discourse as a proof that he was not a man of genius. He earnestly lifted up his voice in public and in private against incompetence and want of intellectual industry in the pulpit. It was his constant endeavor to discourage and suppress the "declamatory raving of ignorance and fanaticism." And he never let pass unimproved any opportunity to rebuke that disposition to noise and disorder, during times of religious interest, which was formerly so common in Liberia. He gave it as his firm and decided intention not to tolerate such undignified proceedings in his church. The friends of reform in this respect must mourn the loss of an efficient and influential co-laborer. May his successor to this charge be blessed with a double portion of his spirit!

Mr. Day was unceasing and untiring in his efforts to promote the educational interests of Liberia generally, and of the Baptist church particularly. It had been, for a series of years, his earnest desire to see a literary institution established in Liberia in connection with the Baptist denomination; and he did not relax his efforts for that purpose until he succeeded in establishing the Day's Hope Academy. Day's Hope! significant appellation! It indicates the deep sentiments of his heart with reference to education. He felt that intellectual and moral culture was the hope of Liberia, of the Church, and of the state; in that were centered all his hopes for the future. May those hopes never be disappointed! May their object be fully and abundantly realized now and hereafter to the latest posterity. We trust that that building and that institution may long remain to proclaim to coming generations the high estimation which their fathers placed upon education. We trust that it will remain to rebuke that false and presumptuous spirit which, while aspiring to usefulness and eminence in the Church and in the state, despises intellectual application! We trust it will remain, with its high and sacred design, to inspire pliant infancy with the desire and disposition to devote themselves to those ennobling pursuits which it was erected to encourage. We trust it will remain, and that in years to come, old age, weary and worn by toil, may be able to look back and be comforted by the reminiscences it shall suggest, and be encouraged by the future it shall indicate! Long may Day's Hope stand! O ye Agents of the Southern Baptist Convention in Liberia and in America! let Day's Hope stand. Let it stand by your fostering care to bless this infant Republic. Let it stand to bless the Church and send forth scores, nay, hundreds of warriors to fight the battles of the Lord; to storm manfully and successfully the numerous fortresses of Satan scattered over this land, and to plant the standard of the cross upon their demolished ruins!

So keenly did Mr. Day appreciate the deficiency of some of the laborers in Christ's vineyard in this land, and so fearful was he lest, in a cause so near and dear to his heart, they, "for want of better mind," should do more evil than good, that very often his references to such and to their labors seemed to those who did not understand him, more the result of a bitter and caustic spirit than of Christian charity. But he earnestly and constantly longed and prayed for, and labored to accelerate, the time when all the pulpits in Liberia, but particularly in his own church, should be filled by "faithful men *able* to teach others."

When we became acquainted with Mr. Day he had already passed the meridian of life. He was what might be called, especially in this country, an old man; but he did not undervalue, as is too often the case with the aged, the improvements of the present day.

> "He looked in years, but in his years were seen
> A youthful vigor, an autumnal green."

While he was no lover of novelty, he always stood ready to adopt and recommend "whatsoever things were true, whatsoever things were lovely, whatsoever things were of good report." He was a man of large experience and extensive reading, and of nice, discriminating judgment. It was not easy to impose upon him. The light and trashy literature of the day, no matter how extolled in newspapers and periodical reviews, found their just deserts when they came into contact with him. He entertained the greatest reverence for the old theological and metaphysical writers. "One line," he would frequently say, "from Edwards, or Butler, or Leighton, or Fuller, is worth pages of many of the productions which the steam-presses so rapidly throw off." He ever referred in most grateful terms to Paley's Natural Theology as having arrested his fearful career, when at one time he was nearing the rapids of skepticism and infidelity. When the illustrious Spurgeon first burst upon the astonished gaze of the Church, extracts from his sermons as reported in newspapers would often be subjected to his cutting severity; but after having received and read several volumes of the sermons of that wonderful young man, his views became considerably modified.

For the last five or six years, and until within a few weeks before his death, as there loomed up in the distance before the faith of this veteran soldier of Christ, the mighty battles that are to be fought and the great victories to be achieved in Africa, he desired to live on indefinitely. He could not fix upon any time in the future in view of the great work to be accomplished, when he would be at leisure to die. Nor was this strange. This is the feeling experienced by most of the aged who have been laboring for the cause of truth and righteousness, when the time draws near to exchange faith for vision, hope for fruition. "The desire for continued existence is a native, ardent, universal passion. It is as inherent and inseparable an attribute of the human soul as the understanding or the will. Christianity adds a religious element, and makes the irrepressible longing a deep and expanded aspiration for an eternal purity, an eternal well-doing and well-being. This passion, when Christianized, is not a simple desire of the spirit for its own endless life in God, but a deep, indwelling interest in the endless life in God of all fellow-spirits. In this way does it become the inspirer of an important religious activity."

This earnest desire for long life Mr. Day experienced, but only that he might exert himself for the glory of God and the benefit of his fellow-men. Hence his activities were unceasing — under all circumstances of health or sickness, if he could only stir. We have frequently seen him wending his weary way to some church-meeting when, judging from his looks, he ought to have been in bed. And we have again and again seen his worn and feeble form in the school-room bending over some obtuse intellect striving to impart an important idea, when he seemed to be in the last stage of debility. And no entreaty of his friends, no admonition of his physician could induce him to relax his labors whenever he felt the least ability to engage in them. He was influenced by a deep conviction that he had a great deal to do and a short time to do it in. In his indefatigable exertions to serve his day and generation, he has left us a noble example:

> "Oh! think how, to his latest day,
> When death, just hovering, claimed his prey
> With Palinure's unaltered mood,
> Firm at his dangerous post he stood;
> Each call for needful rest repelled,
> With dying hand the rudder held,
> Till, in his fall, with fateful sway,
> The steerage of the realm gave way."

A few months previous to his last illness he seemed to have conceived a presentiment of the approach of his latter end. But he did not as usual express any desire to live. He seemed to have no fears at all of dying. He viewed death and spoke of his own dissolution with perfect indifference — not, indeed, with the indifference of the stoic, but with the composure and unruffled calmness peculiar to the Christian.

On Sunday, the sixth of February, he came, as was his custom when able to walk, to this house, where a large and eager congregation was anxiously waiting to hear the words of wisdom and counsel which were wont to fall from his lips. He conducted the preliminary exercises with his usual ease and dignity; but, alas! the "silver cord was loosed," and his audience knew it not. When he arose to announce his text, he was seized with such weakness as rendered him wholly unable to proceed. Having been taken home, he went to bed, but from that bed he rose no more. On the fifteenth of February his spirit was summoned to eternal realities. The last assembly he met on earth was an assembly of God's people, with whom he was essaying to worship. In a few days after, his spirit mingled with that illustrious and noble army of martyrs who

> ——"shine
> With robes of victory through the skies."

We had not the opportunity of being at his bed-side immediately before his death, and we can not accurately give you his dying words. But we know that it was a privilege to be there, for

> "The chamber where the good man meets his fate
> Is privileged beyond the common walks of life,
> Quite on the verge of heaven."

We know that he was not at all dismayed as he stood, conscious of approaching dissolution, on the very verge of eternity. Oh! no. But over its dark and untraveled vastness he cast a fearless eye; and, as he saw himself hastening

> ——"to join
> The innumerable caravan that moves
> To the pale realms of shade, where each shall take
> His chamber in the silent halls of death,
> He went not like the quarry slave at night,
> Scourged to his dungeon; but, sustained and soothed
> By an unfaltering trust, approached his grave,
> Like one who wraps the drapery of his couch
> About him and lies down to pleasant dreams."

Mr. Day is gone! Never more will his voice be heard within these walls. Never more will he lift up the voice of warning to the impenitent and administer encouragement and comfort to the desponding believer. Never more will he mingle in the public councils of the nation and assist, by his presence and instruction, in the various enterprises of popular interest. He is gone — from the Church and state! Hear it, ye aged fathers! and strive to do with all your might whatsoever your hands find to do. Hear it, O cheerful youth! and lay aside your trifling hilarity, and think of the responsibilities which must soon fall upon you, and endeavor to qualify yourselves for their assumption.

While, however, the death of Mr. Day has occasioned an irreparable loss to Church and state, we do not feel to entertain unmingled emotions of sorrow. He has left us an illustrious example. We have reasons for congratulations in view of the noble instance afforded for the contemplation of the world, the encouragement of the Church, and the emulation of the rising generation, of a long life of self-denial and usefulness closed with a beautiful serenity — a dignified calmness and peace. Such a life, such a death, constitute a legacy richer than the silver mines of Peru, and more valuable than the sparkling deposits of Australia or California. Let us avail ourselves of it.

> "Lives of great men all remind us,
> We can make our lives sublime;
> And, departing, leave behind us
> Footprints on the sand of time."

A CHAPTER

IN THE

HISTORY OF THE AFRICAN SLAVE-TRADE.

A Chapter in the History of the African Slave-Trade.*

"*Quæ cura ora eruoris nostro?*"—Hor. 11 B. Ode I.

THE great epochs of the history, whether of mankind generally or of one particular section of the human race, are not unusually preceded by occurrences more or less extraordinary. These occurrences, cursorily viewed, inspire opinions as to their ultimate results, which subsequent experience and the development of the results themselves prove to have been entirely erroneous. And often what would seem to be the natural and necessary interpretation of the tendency of any particular train of events is discovered to be as wide from the truth as possible. Hence, while there may be formed the most plausible conjectures as to the true character and bearing of any given circumstance or combination of circumstances, the uncertainty of results necessarily precludes the possibility of a just appreciation of any event at the time of its occurrence. The hatred which we learn from sacred story existed in the large family of Jewish brothers against one of their number, upon whom the head of the family seemed to lavish all the affection of old age, the bitterness with which they persecuted him, and the unnatural and cruel indifference with which they consigned him to slavery, were circumstances which seemed to justify the anticipation that the object of their malignity would

* Reprinted from the *Anglo-African* for June, 1859.

suffer, pine away, and die in miserable obscurity. But his bondage was the means, humanly speaking, of introducing him to a position, whence, in after-years during a period of pressing exigency, he could administer to the relief and deliverance of the whole family. So before the permanent establishment of the nation whom God had chosen to be the depositary of his will and to preserve a knowledge of himself, amid the general apostasy of mankind; whose conservative character was to influence either remotely or directly other portions of the human family, they must go down into Egypt, and there, in a land of strangers, be afflicted "four hundred years;" their moral and intellectual powers must pass under the withering and blighting influence of a pernicious bondage; circumstances which seemed entirely at variance with the preparation required by a people destined to occupy the high and important position which the Jews afterwards filled in the world. So also when there was to be established the nation whom God had chosen to "conquer the world and subject it to the dominion of law," as preparatory to the advent of the "Prince of Peace," one of the most ancient and powerful states must pass through a series of unprecedented calamities, and, at length, leveled to the dust by the "unsparing steel and devouring element," of relentless foes, from its ashes must spring forth the germ of the chosen people—the all-conquering Romans.

—— "Res Asiae Priamique evertere gentem
Immeritam visum Superis.*

So, again, in modern times, when the period draws near for the redemption and delivery of Africa from the

* Virgil's Æneid. B. III. 1.

barbarism and degradation of unnumbered years, there must take place circumstances so horrible in their character, and so revolting to the nobler instincts of man as to find few disposed to recognize in them the hand of a supreme and merciful Ruler.

"Sunt lachrymæ rerum, et mentem mortalia tangunt."

Almost coëval with the invention of printing and the discovery of America—two great eras in the history of human improvement — was the beginning of the African slave-trade. As soon as the empire of Europe, following the guiding "star" of destiny, began to move "westward," she dragged Africa, rather tardy in the march of nations, along with her to the place which seems to have been designed for the rejuvenescence of eastern senility, for the untrammeled exercise and healthful growth of the principles of political and ecclesiastical liberty, and for the more thorough development of man. And it can not be denied that the Africans when first carried to the Western world were benefited. The men under whose tutelage they were taken generally regarded them as a solemn charge intrusted to their care by Providence, and felt bound to instruct them, and in every way to ameliorate their condition. They were not only indoctrinated into the principles of Christianity, but they were taught the arts and sciences. The relation of the European to the African in those unsophisticated times was that of guardian and *protégé*. And the system, if slavery it was, bore a strong resemblance to slavery as it existed among the Romans, in the earlier periods of their history, when the "slave was the teacher, the artist, the actor, the man of science, the physician." Hence many good men, in view of the benefits which they saw accrue from the mild and generous system, embarked their capital in, and gave their influence to, the enterprise of transporting negroes from Africa. The virulent features of the trade were not developed until the enormous gains which were found to result from the toil of the African and the consequent demand for his labor, had supplied the Western continent with hordes of these children of the sun. But the evils of the system, though horrifying in the extreme, were not regarded of sufficient magnitude to arrest the importation of slaves. The benefits which the poor heathen received in his deportation from a land of barbarism to a land of civilization furnished a counterbalancing argument to the mind of those benevolent souls who were actively engaged in the trade — the rapidity and ease with which they were enriching their coffers was, of course, only incidental to their glorious design of civilizing poor, benighted Africa!!

But it was not long before the true character of the traffic began unmistakably to discover itself. Its immense gains brought men of various characters into competition. The whole western coast of Africa became the haunt of the slave-trader, and the scene of unutterable cruelties as the result of their operations. The more powerful native chiefs, impelled by those sordid and cruel feelings which, in the absence of higher motives, actuate men, made war upon their weaker neighbors in order to capture prisoners to supply the demand of the traders; and a state of things was induced which awakened the commiseration and called forth the remonstrances of the thoughtful and philanthropic in Christian lands. Wilberforce, Granville Sharp, and others, ably exhibited before the British public the horrible effects of the trade; pointed out its disastrous influence upon the peaceful communities of Africa; showed its agency in the disintegration of African society, and in the feuds and guerrillas which distracted the African coast; discovered it as depopulating the continent, and giving rise to multifarious and indescribable evils; and proposed as a remedy the immediate abolition of the traffic. In 1792 Mr. H. Thornton, Chairman of the Sierra Leone Company, said, in the course of a discussion consequent upon a motion made by Mr. Wilberforce for the abolition of the slave-trade: "It had obtained the name of a *trade;* and many had been deceived by the appellation; but it was a war, not a *trade;* it was a *mass of crimes*, and not *commerce;* it alone prevented the introduction of trade into Africa. It created more embarrassments than all the natural impediments of the country, and was more hard to contend with than any difficulties of climate, soil, or natural dispositions of the people." The slave-traders by pampering their cupidity had so ingratiated themselves with the native rulers of the country, and had acquired such an influence on the coast, that nothing could be suffered which would at all interfere with the activity of the trade. The establishment of any settlement or colony opposed to the traffic was of course out of the question.

The close of the eighteenth century, when experience had proved the traffic to be at variance with the laws of God and an outrage upon humanity, witnessed the inauguration of vigorous efforts on the part of the philanthropists in England for the destruction of its legality. Mr. Wilberforce, having introduced the motion in Parliament " that the trade carried on by British subjects for the purpose of obtaining slaves on the African coast ought to be abolished," the friends of the motion ceased not in their efforts until on the tenth of February, 1807, a committee of the whole House passed a bill "that no vessel should clear out for slaves from any port within the British dominions after May 1, 1807," fifteen years after the introduction of Mr. Wilberforce's motion. The legality of the traffic being thus overthrown by England, and by other nations following in her wake, the horrors of the traffic manifestly declined, and honorable commerce could again be prosecuted with some measure of safety.

The temporary immunity of the coast from the horrors attendant upon the slave-trade, occasioned by the passage of the British "Abolition Act," furnished an opportunity to certain philanthropists in America to carry out an idea which had originated years previously, of planting on the west coast of Africa a colony of civilized Africans, but which had seemed impracticable in consequence of the unlimited and pernicious sway which the slavers held on the coast. In the year 1816 a Society was instituted under the denomination of the "American Colonization Society," for the purpose of colonizing in Africa, with their own consent, free persons of color of the United States. In 1820, the necessary preparations having been made, the ship Elizabeth sailed from the United States with a company of eighty-eight emigrants for the west coast of Africa. After various trials and difficulties they landed on Cape Monserrado and succeeded in establishing themselves. But scarcely had they intrenched themselves when the slavers, a few of whom still hovered on the coast and had factories in the vicinity of Monserrado, began to manifest their hostility to the settlers, endeavoring in every possible way to break up the settlement; while the aboriginal neighbors of the colonists, finding that the presence of the colony was diminishing very considerably their gains from the unhallowed trade, indulged a lurking enmity which only awaited opportunity to develop itself. But the opportunity was not long in offering, for the colony was hardly two years old when it was desperately assailed by untold numbers of savages who came down in wild ferocity upon the feeble and defenseless company, and must have swept away every trace of them had not a merciful Providence vouchsafed deliverance to the weak. The settlers triumphed against overwhelming odds.

The slave-traders, notwithstanding the signal defeat of their native allies in the traffic, were not willing to abandon a scene which for scores of years they had unmolestedly and profitably infested. They still lingered about the settlement. "From eight to ten, and even fifteen vessels were engaged at the same time in this odious traffic almost under the guns of the settlement; and in July of the same year, (1825,) contracts were existing for eight hundred slaves to be furnished in the short space of four months, within eight miles of the Cape. Four hundred of these were to be purchased for two American traders."* During the same year Mr. Ashmun, agent of the American Colonization Society, wrote to the Society: "The colony only wants the right; it has the power to expel this traffic to a distance, and force it at least to conceal some of its worst enormities." From this time the Society began to take into consideration the importance of enlarging the territory of the colony, and thus including within its jurisdiction several tribes, in order both to protect the settlement against the evil of too great proximity to slave-factories and to place it within the competency of

* Gurley's *Life of Ashmun*, page 261.

the colonial authorities to "expel the traffic to a distance." But even after the limits of the colony had been greatly extended and several large tribes brought under its jurisdiction, the slavers would every now and then attempt to renew their old friendships, and frequently occasioned not a little trouble to the colonists by exciting the natives to insubordination and hostility to a colony which, as they alleged, (being instructed so to think by the slavers,) "was spoiling their country and breaking up their lucrative trade."

The feelings of some of the natives who had surrendered themselves to Liberian authority, became, under the guidance of the "marauding outlaws," so embittered against the colony that they more than once boldly avowed their hostile sentiments, and professed utter indifference to the laws of Liberia. This, together with the fact that every once in a while slavers would locate themselves, erect barracoons and purchase slaves on Liberian territory under the countenance and protection of aboriginal chiefs, rendered several wars (?) against the latter necessary in order to convince them that Liberians had power to compel them to obedience. The last war of this character was "carried" to New-Cess in 1849, immediately after the independence of Liberia had been recognized by England and France. The condign punishment inflicted upon the slavers by that military expedition, the regular cruising of the Liberian government schooner Lark, and the scattering of settlements at various points, have entirely driven away the slavers from the Liberian coast. The country in consequence has enjoyed a grateful repose, and the people have been peaceably prosecuting a legitimate traffic both with Liberians and foreigners.

But latterly a new element of discord has been introduced on the Liberian coast, the French emigration system. French vessels visit the coast for the ostensible object of employing laborers for the French colonies. Of course it is understood or presumed that all emigrants embarking on board of these vessels do so of their own accord; if so, the trade is as lawful as any other emigration trade. But it must be borne in mind that the aborigines are not settled along the coast in independent republican communities. They are under the most despotic rule; the king or head-man having absolute control over his subjects or "boys." All the employer of emigrants has to do, then, is to offer, which he does, liberal conditions to the chiefs for the number of laborers required. The chiefs immediately send around and compel their boys to come, or if they have not a sufficient number of their own people to answer the demand, predatory excursions are made, in which they kidnap the weak and unsuspecting, or a pretext is assumed for a war with a neighboring tribe; cruelty, bloodshed, carnage ensue; prisoners are taken, driven down to the beach and handed over to the captain of the emigrant ship, whose business being to employ all the laborers he can get, does not stop to inquire as to the method adopted for obtaining these persons. The result is, a state of things as revolting as that occasioned by the slave-trade in its most flourishing period. The bond which it was hoped Liberia had formed for the linking together of tribe to tribe in harmonious intercourse and mutual dependence, is thus being rudely snapped asunder. The natives, according to complaints made by some of them to the Liberian government, are being agitated with reciprocal fears and jealousies, their lives and property are in danger, and a check is imposed upon all their industrious efforts.

An occurrence, however, sad indeed, but no doubt providential, has recently taken place on the Liberian coast, which has clearly developed the character of the system, and which will, in all probability, arrest its deleterious influences. In the early part of April last (1858) the Regina Coeli, a French ship engaged in the enlistment of laborers, as above stated, was laying at anchor off Manna, a trading port a few leagues northwest of Monrovia, with two or three hundred emigrants on board, among whom, in consequence of some of their number being manacled, considerable dissatisfaction prevailed. During the absence of the captain and one of the officers, a quarrel broke out between the cook and one of the emigrants. The cook struck the emigrant, the latter retaliated, when a scuffle ensued, in which other emigrants took part. This attracted the attention of the rest of the crew, who coming to the assistance of the cook, violently beat the emigrants, killing several of them. By this time, those emigrants who had been confined below were unshackled, and joining in the fracas killed in retaliation all the crew, save one man who fled aloft and protested most earnestly his freedom from any participation in the matter. The emigrants, recognizing his innocence, spared his life, but ordered him ashore forthwith, which order he readily obeyed.

The surviving emigrants having sole charge of the vessel, awaited the arrival of the captain to dispatch him as soon as he touched the deck. But he, learning their design, did not venture on board, but sought and obtained aid from the Liberian authorities at Cape Mount to keep the exasperated savages from stranding his vessel. The unfortunate ship was subsequently rescued by an English mail steamer, and towed into Monserrado Roads.

One very important result has accrued from this sad occurrence, and that is the one already referred to—the development of the ruinous influence of the French emigration system upon the natives from among whom the laborers are taken. There have existed apprehensions on the part of the Liberian government that the emigration was constrained; but having received official information and assurance that the system enjoyed the countenance and patronage of the French government, and that the traders were under the immediate surveillance of French officials, it could not depreciate the honesty and good intentions of that renowned and magnanimous nation.

Nearly coincident with the above circumstance, and, perhaps, in some measure the result of it, was another of a similar character, in the interior of Liberia. One or two native chiefs, it appears, had collected a number of persons and were conveying them, manacled, to the coast for the purpose of supplying the emigrant vessels. On their way they stopped, with their human load, to pass the night at a native town. During the night, one of the captives having worked himself loose, untied the others, when a revolt ensued in which the prisoners killed their kidnappers and made their escape.

It is a matter of profound regret that such should be the concomitants of a system which was doubtless designed by the French government for the benefit of the African race, and which, if judiciously carried out, according to its original intention, would probably result in the downfall of American slavery. A French periodical published in Paris, states the view taken of the system by French philanthropists as follows:

"La France, en agissant comme elle le fait, ne travaille pas seulement pour la fortune des deux îles qui lui restent dans l'archipel des petites

Antilles; elle a, il est vrai, a peupler aussi, dans le cercle plus spécial des intérets nationaux, la Guyane française et l'Algérie; mais elle a surtout la mission de protéger de son pavillon et de couronner de son auréole morale une œuvre essentiellement humanitaire, dont la double conséquence doit être, d'extirper l'esclavage de deux continents a la fois, de l'Afrique et de l'Amérique."*

If the emigration system could be carried on without involving the coast in such fearful distractions, it would, we are inclined to believe, furnish before long a fair and satisfactory solution of the problem respecting the comparative productiveness of slave and free labor. There would be furnished in Guiana and other French colonies, to which these emigrants are taken, an example of vast tropical regions extensively and profitably cultivated by hordes of free native Africans. But so long as the system bears a compulsory character, the results to Africa of the efforts of those engaged in it, can not fail to be disastrous. And no intercourse of foreigners with the natives, in the vicinity of Liberia and Sierra Leone, containing in it any element of the slave-trade, will be long endured. Through the influence of these civilized and Christian colonies, the natives far and near have been taught the sacredness of human rights. They will not easily and silently submit to enslavement, if there is the least chance of successful resistance. From Sierra Leone to Bereby, a distance of about seven hundred miles of coast, with an interior of about one hundred and fifty miles, and a population of about eight hundred thousand souls, the natives have caught the inspiration of the Genius of universal Freedom, and they too sing—

"Hereditary bondmen, know ye not,
That they who would be free, themselves must strike the blow!"

In a great part of this region, what is an unmistaka-

* *Annales d'Afrique, Mars et Avril*, 1858.

ble indication that the natives have permanently abandoned the slave-trade, is the absence of barricaded towns, which formerly, when the trade was rife, were indispensable to their protection from the slave-hunters. And these sentiments of freedom are spreading themselves far and wide, into the equatorial regions of Africa. Besides the influence which the missionaries scattered along the coast for about two thousand miles, are exerting, " a commencement has been made of home migration of liberated Africans, from Sierra Leone into the Yoruba country." These people having received an education under the operation of the free principles of English law, and having accumulated a little property, are returning home deeply imbued with a sense of the wrong and injustice of the slave-trade, and are forming settlements on civilized and Christian principles. The ardent and enlightened love of liberty, which has been engendered among them, under the teachings of those friends of the African, will render them anxious not only to reduce to practice, but widely to disseminate those lessons of personal and political liberty. And it may reasonably be hoped, that they will soon so generally diffuse their principles among the natives of those regions, so develop and strengthen among the masses the love of freedom, as to render those chiefs who favor the slave-trade, unpopular among their people, as all such miscreants are becoming in the vicinity of Liberia.

The unusual rush recently made by slavers to certain portions of the equatorial coast, have called for vigorous action on the part of the British squadron, which has resulted in the capture of several notorious slavers. The American squadron, which has hitherto not been as efficient as desirable, is now on the alert. Measures are taking, we understand, to increase the efficiency of this squadron. From the coöperation of the two squadrons, much good may be expected, or rather we may look for the prevention of much evil.

But while the odious traffic is receiving its death-wounds on the coast, we hear of a determination on the part of some in North-America to resuscitate it. Upon almost every wind that sweeps from the United States do we receive indications of a disposition in certain sections of that country to commence the importation of slaves into the Southern States. In the reports of Congress and State Legislatures, in the public newspapers, in the sermons of eminent divines, in private letters, we have the same admonition. One may *aspectu primo* be somewhat surprised to find such a feeling existing in a land, which in point of intellectual and moral light, is among the most favored in the world. But when it is considered that we have fallen upon times when "the lust of gain is the sole impulse of human activity, and almost the only umpire of human life," when intellect has become the slave of avarice, though proclaiming its incontestable dominion over the universe, we can hardly wonder. It is by no means surprising that there should be such a failure on the part of those votaries of slavery and the slave-trade, in the land of light, to discover that flagrant wrong and enormous guilt involved in their favorite pursuit; for, besides the strenuous efforts which they make to believe and to disseminate the dogma that "the black man has no rights which white men are bound to respect," their indisposition to work with their own hands, and the prodigious gains which accrue to them from the unrecompensed toil of the Negro, have erected an insurmountable and impenetrable barrier between them and RIGHT. "I can never cease to be most unfeignedly thankful," says Dr. Livingstone, "that I was not born in a land of slaves. No one can understand the effect of the unutterable meanness of the slave system on the minds of those who, but for the strange obliquity which prevents them from feeling the degradation of not being gentlemen enough to pay for services rendered, would be equal in virtue to ourselves. Fraud becomes as natural to them as 'paying one's way' is to the rest of mankind."*

But we are rather encouraged than otherwise by the noisy boasting of the pro-slavery zealots. We regard it, all things considered, as a favorable augury. It is our deliberate opinion that, if the real feelings of some of the loudest defenders of slavery were known, we should find them briefly but truly expressed in the significant device: "Le passé me tourmente, et je crains l'avenir."

The days of giant oppression are numbered and he knows it. His hideous and menacing roars are only accompaniments of his dying paroxysms. While we must admit that the "gnashing of his teeth," and his "horrible grins," are indications of what he would do under more favorable circumstances, yet, knowing as we do, the march of events in the current history of the world, we can not but regard it as a sign of supervening enervation and overwhelming overthrow.

* *Livingstone's Miss. Travels, &c., in South-Africa*, p. 89.

www.ingramcontent.com/pod-product-compliance
Lightning Source LLC
Chambersburg PA
CBHW030249170426
43202CB00009B/685